# INTRODUCTION

Crop circles also known as "Agrograms" or "Agroglyphs" are a phenomena that has captivated human curiosity for centuries, appearing overnight in fields and inspiring countless theories and debates about their origins and purpose that persist to this day. This book presents compelling evidence that a significant number of these crop circle patterns may be the product of contact with a higher intelligence.

Among the most intriguing formations are those such as the repeating "Hydrogen Signature" and the 2001 "Arecibo Response". The Hydrogen Signature is particularly significant because it aligns with what we might expect in communication from a higher intelligence, echoing principles used by SETI. The Arecibo Response stands out as a direct reply to a human-initiated message, demonstrating precisely what we might expect to receive from an extraterrestrial civilization or otherwise higher intelligent lifeform.

The choice of crops as a medium for these messages is both novel and ingenious. Unlike radio waves, which could interfere with our communications and reveal an origin location of the signal, crop circles offer a non-intrusive, untraceable and pictorial method of conveying information. This method requires a level of technical advancement and a deep understanding of both our technological capabilities and the environment, suggesting the existence of a higher intelligence that is aware of our limitations and communicates in a way that seeks to minimize disruption to the function of humanity.

The methods that a higher intelligence might use to contact us could be so alien that we fail to recognize it as communication. Using crops to create intricate patterns can be likened to how we might attempt to communicate with species we consider less intelligent, such as chimpanzees or dogs. Just as we use visual symbols and basic tools to engage with animals, these crop circles could be the equivalent from a more advanced intelligence reaching out to humanity. This approach respects our current technological level while encouraging us to decipher and understand the messages conveyed through these remarkable formations. Consider how important food is to us and how difficult it would be to ignore these patterns appearing in our source of food. but in a way that also gives human authorities a level of plausible deniability.

This book raises major questions about the crop circle phenomenon as a whole, strongly suggesting the existence of two separate phenomena: man-made art (either as a passion project or a cover-up operation) and genuine signals from a higher intelligence. The exploration of crop circles in this book aims to differentiate between these two phenomena. While acknowledging the role of human hoaxers, it delves into the evidence that supports the theory of higher intelligence origins. Many of the patterns suggest makers possess knowledge and technology that would be extraordinarily difficult, if not impossible, for human hoaxers to replicate convincingly. Additionally, formations like the blueprint series and the signal device depictions hint at advanced technological concepts that are beyond our current understanding.

Adding to the credibility of the existence of potential extraterrestrial contact in general, former intelligence officer David Grusch's testimony to Congress has confirmed the recovery of "non-human biologics" from crashed UFOs. This along with prior Pentagon releases acknowledging the existence of Unidentified Aerial Phenomena (UAPs), solidifies the reality of an extraterrestrial presence of some kind on Earth. This also raises profound questions not only about our place in the universe, but also about the 70+ year cover up campaign of the UFO phenomena by authorities. Naturally extending to questions about its similarities to the crop circle phenomena, which is itself often associated with the sighting of UFOs.

These recent developments make the study of crop circles far more pertinent in my view. If extraterrestrial beings or a higher intelligence of some kind are indeed trying to communicate, crop circles might be the most tangible evidence we have of their presence and intentions. The layers of meaning, precise geometry, mathematical significance, and symbolic meanings of these formations do indeed hint at a sophisticated form of contact, urging us to look closer and understand the messages appearing in our fields.

This book also provides a comprehensive overview of the crop circle phenomena, presenting the case for their potential origins as messages from a higher intelligence. It sets the foundation for further research and analysis, encouraging readers to consider and take seriously the possibility that we are actively being contacted by a higher intelligence and that here is, in fact, the signal that SETI has been searching for.

# CHAPTER 1: THE HISTORY OF THE CROP CIRCLE PHENOMENA

While modern crop circle encounters have brought significant attention and speculation, historical accounts suggest that these enigmatic formations have been appearing in our fields for much longer. This chapter delves into the historical records and folklore surrounding crop circles, tracing their origins from ancient times to the early modern phenomena.

## ANCIENT & MEDIEVAL ACCOUNTS

### Early Mentions and Folklore
Crop circles, or at least their precursors, have been documented in various forms throughout history. Some of the earliest references can be found in the folklore and myths of different cultures. Ancient texts and oral traditions often describe strange patterns appearing in fields, sometimes attributed to divine or supernatural forces.

### The Mowing Devil
One of the most famous early accounts of a crop circle dates back to 1678 in England. A woodcut pamphlet titled "The Mowing Devil" depicts a demon-like figure cutting a circular pattern in a field of oats. The accompanying text tells the story of a farmer who, after refusing to pay a laborer to mow his field, swore he would rather have the devil himself do the work. That night, the field was found to have been mysteriously mowed in a perfect circle, suggesting otherworldly involvement.

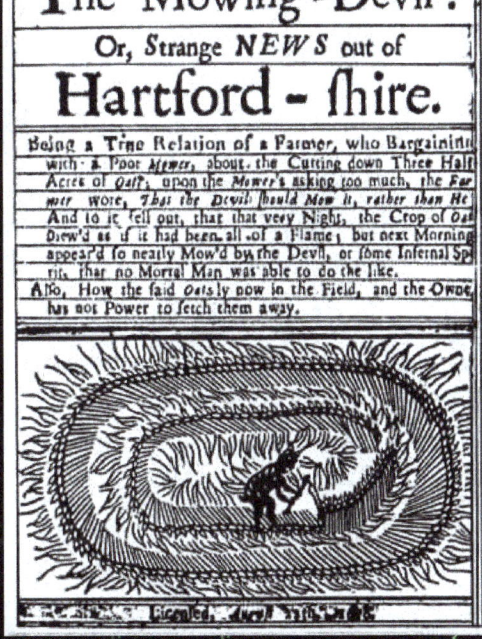

The pamphlet's transcription reads as follows:
"The Mowing-Devil: Or, Strange NEWS out of Hartford-shire. Being a True Relation of a Farmer, who Bargaining with a poor Mower, about the Cutting down Three Half Acres of Oats upon the Mower's asking too much, the Farmer swore, 'That the Devil should Mow it, rather than He.' And lo it fell out, that that very Night, the Crop of Oats shew'd as if it had been all of a Flame, but next Morning appear'd so neatly Mow'd by the Devil, or some Infernal Spirit, that no Mortal Man was able to do the like. Also, How the said Oats ly now in the Field, and the Owner has not Power to fetch them away."

This account is particularly intriguing because of its clear descriptions, which parallel modern observations of crop circles:
- The phrase "so neatly Mow'd by the Devil, or some Infernal Spirit, that no Mortal Man was able to do the like" echoes modern sentiments that the precision of crop circles cannot be replicated by human hands.
- The reference to the crop appearing "as if it had been all of a Flame" suggests a potential link to the light orb phenomenon reported in modern crop circle encounters.
- Finally, the area in which this was recorded matches that of the majority of modern day crop circle occurrances.

## EARLY SCIENTIFIC OBSERVATIONS

### Robert Plot's Writings
In the late 17th century, Robert Plot, a naturalist and the first Professor of Chemistry at the University of Oxford, documented several instances of unusual circular patterns in fields. In his book "The Natural History of Staffordshire" (1686), Plot describes these formations in detail, speculating that they could be caused by lightning strikes or other natural phenomena. While his explanations leaned towards natural causes, the detailed documentation provided early scientific recognition of crop circles.

### The Connection with Weather Phenomena
Throughout history, it would seem that many crop circles have been mistaken for weather-related phenomena. Early observers often attributed the formations to whirlwinds or a phenomena known as "fairy rings", caused by

fungal growth, or other natural events. These explanations persisted for centuries, especially as crop circles were relatively simple in design and could be plausibly linked to environmental causes.

## The Light Orb Phenomena

Historical accounts occasionally mention strange lights or orbs in conjunction with crop circles. These sightings, often described as glowing balls of light hovering above fields, were considered omens or supernatural events in many cultures. The light orb phenomenon remains a point of interest in modern crop circle research, suggesting a potential link between the formations and unexplained aerial phenomena.

## The Mystery of the White Horses

Another fascinating aspect of crop circle history is their connection to the chalk white horses of England. These large hill figures, carved into the landscape to reveal the white chalk beneath, have been linked to the crop circle phenomenon. The most famous of these, such as the Uffington White Horse, date back to prehistoric times. Interestingly, many crop circles have been found within 50 miles of Stonehenge which is also the case for these mysterious ancient carvings of unknown origin.

The origins of these white horses are shrouded in mystery. While they are often attributed to ancient peoples and cultures, the exact purpose and creators remain unknown. This ambiguity parallels the enigma of crop circles. Some theories suggest that both phenomena may be connected, possibly as part of a larger, hidden historical narrative involving advanced knowledge or extraterrestrial influences.

The controversy around the recorded history of these figures is also noteworthy. Scholars and historians often debate the true meanings and origins of the white horses, sometimes suggesting that historical records have been misinterpreted or manipulated. This controversy echoes the skepticism and debate surrounding crop circles. The fact that the white horses in the same geographical areas in which crop circles frequently appear, adds an intriguing layer of mystery and potential connection between the crop circle phenomena and the existence of the white horses.

## The Evolution of Crop Circles

As we move from ancient times to the early modern period, it becomes evident that crop circles have evolved in both frequency and complexity. Historical records, though sporadic, indicate that these formations were not entirely unheard of but were often dismissed as curiosities or attributed to folklore. The increasing documentation in the 17th and 18th centuries marked a shift towards a more systematic observation of these mysterious patterns.

## The History of Crop Circles

The history of crop circles is rich with intriguing stories and observations that span centuries. From ancient myths and medieval pamphlets to early scientific investigations, these formations have captured human imagination and curiosity long before they became a modern phenomenon. Understanding this historical context is important as we explore the more recent and complex manifestations of crop circles in the subsequent chapters. This journey through history sets the stage for a deeper exploration of the crop circle phenomena and its potential implications for our understanding of the world and the possibility of extraterrestrial contact.

THE UFFINGTON CHALK WHITE HORSE, OXFORDSHIRE
ONE OF 16 CHALK WHITE HORSES IN SOUTH-WEST UK

# CHAPTER 2: EARLY MODERN CROP CIRCLE OCCURRANCES

The late 20th century saw a significant resurgence in crop circle activity, leading to heightened interest and investigation. This chapter explores the early modern encounters with crop circles, their increasing complexity, some theories, and the impact of media coverage on public perception.

## LATE 1970'S AND EARLY 1980'S

The resurgence of crop circles in the late 1970s and early 1980s marked a new chapter in their history. Early reports from England, particularly in Wiltshire, documented strange patterns appearing in fields. One notable example is the Westbury White Horse, a famous chalk figure in Wiltshire where crop circles were reported. Farmers and locals observed perfect circles appearing in the fields, leading to curiosity and concern.

**Early Formations**
The crop circles of this period were relatively simple in design, often consisting of basic circles or rings. These early formations captured public attention but did not yet exhibit the complexity that would characterize later crop circle formations.

**Potential Sabotage Operations and Controversies**
During this early phase, there was controversy regarding the lack of sophisticated patterns akin to those seen later. There was some clear evidence that some patterns had been sabotaged during this time, something that could be ongoing, This period can be likened to a "telephone call dialing," where initial patterns were simple and repetitive, evolving in complexity over time, akin to when the person answers the call. Some suggest this simplicity might have been a deliberate strategy to gradually prepare observers for more intricate designs. There exists some evidence suggesting that Cambridge University might have created one of the early Mandelbrot formations. This involvement could have been an exercise in advanced mathematics, part of a covert operation or just a simple prank.

# THE "WOW!" SIGNAL & CROP CIRCLE CONNECTION

In 1977, astronomer Jerry R. Ehman detected a brief but intense radio signal from space while working at Ohio State University's Big Ear radio telescope. The signal, known as the "Wow!" signal, was a 72-second burst of radio waves from the direction of the Sagittarius constellation. The signal was highly unusual and has been the subject of much speculation regarding its potential extraterrestrial origin due to its high intensity burst and its frequency being at the 1420mhz Hydrogen line.

**Potential Link to Crop Circle Phenomena**

The emergence of crop circles shortly after the Wow! signal presents an intriguing correlation. The "Wow!" signal was a significant event in the search for extraterrestrial intelligence (SETI), representing a potential first contact with other intelligent life. The timing of the crop circle phenomena, beginning in the late 1970s, suggests a link between these occurrences.

We could propose that the increase in crop circle activity may be a form of response or communication attempt from a higher intelligence following the "Wow!" signal. The initial simple patterns of crop circles might be interpreted as a preliminary attempt at communication, evolving in complexity as the phenomenon gained more attention and as technological and scientific understanding progressed.

This connection raises intriguing questions about the nature of crop circles and whether they could be linked to a broader attempt at extraterrestrial communication or a follow up to the "Wow!" signal. The timing and evolution of crop circles, paired with the dramatic nature of the "Wow!" signal, support the hypothesis that both phenomena might be part of a larger, interconnected communication effort.

**THE ORIGINAL "WOW!" SIGNAL PRINT OUT WITH THE HIGH INTENSITY READINGS OUTLINED**

# INCREASING COMPLEXITY

### Transition to Intricate Designs
By the late 1980's and early 1990's, the complexity of crop circles began to increase dramatically. Patterns evolved from simple circles to elaborate geometric shapes, fractals, and other mathematically significant forms. Notable examples from this period include formations resembling the "Julia Set" and "Mandelbrot Set," which showcased a level of sophistication that challenged earlier explanations.

### Notable Examples
The "Julia Set" (1996) pattern, for instance, displayed a complex fractal design that required precise geometric understanding. Similarly, the "Mandelbrot Set" (1990) pattern, which is a well-known fractal, demonstrated an advanced level of mathematical complexity. There was also the pattern used for the Led Zepplin album cover in 1990 and the Barbury Castle trinary formation in 1991, still of unknown meaning. These patterns were not only larger and more intricate but also exhibited a level of precision that was difficult to achieve by manual means, leading to increased speculation about their origins.

# EARLY THEORIES & INVESTIGATIONS OF NATURAL PHENOMENA

### Meteorological Theories
In the early stages of modern crop circle research, meteorological explanations were prominent. Theories suggested that whirlwinds, plasma vortexes, and other weather-related phenomena could create circular patterns in fields. These explanations were based on observable natural phenomena and were initially used to account for the simpler crop patterns.

### Limitations
As crop circles became more complex, these meteorological explanations began to fall short. The intricate designs and precise geometrical patterns observed in later crop circles could not be fully explained by simple weather phenomena, prompting researchers to seek alternative explanations.

## THE HUMAN HOAXES EXPLAINATION

### Doug Bower and Dave Chorley
At the end of the 1991 crop circle season Doug and Dave publicly claimed responsibility for many of the early crop circles in the late 1980's. They demonstrated their technique using planks and ropes, which seemed to support the hoax theory. Their claims led to widespread belief that many crop circles were the result of human activity.

### Challenges to the Hoax Theory
Despite Bower and Chorley's claims, there were numerous crop circles that exhibited complexities and characteristics difficult to replicate by human hands. The size, scale, and intricacy of some formations, along with the rapid appearance overnight and the absence of footprints or other signs of human activity, raised questions about the validity of the hoax theory. Additionally, the high frequency and sporadic, global distribution of crop circles suggested that the phenomena might not be entirely explained by just human pranksters.

## MEDIA COVERAGE, PUBLIC PERCEPTION & THE ROLE OF MEDIA

### Early Media Reports
The media played a crucial role in shaping public perception of crop circles. Early reports often treated crop circles as curiosities or local oddities, but as the phenomena persisted and grew more complex, media coverage became more serious and widespread. Television documentaries, newspaper articles, and radio shows began to explore the mystery, interviewing witnesses and researchers.

### Impact on Public Perception
The increased media attention brought crop circles into the mainstream consciousness, leading to a surge in public interest. This interest was further fueled by the contrasting theories about their origins, from natural phenomena and human hoaxes to extraterrestrial involvement. The mystery and allure of crop circles captured the imagination of the public, turning fields of crops into sites of pilgrimage for enthusiasts and researchers alike.

# INFLUENTIAL MEDIA MOMENTS

### Television and Documentaries
Several television documentaries in the late 20th century significantly impacted public perception. Programs such as the BBC's "Out of This World" and "Arthur C. Clarke's Mysterious World" presented crop circles as phenomena worthy of scientific investigation, often featuring interviews with experts who provided various explanations.

### Newspaper Coverage
National and local newspapers frequently reported on new crop circle formations, often highlighting the most intricate and mysterious examples. Headlines ranged from skeptical accounts of hoaxes to speculative pieces about possible extraterrestrial messages.

# EVOLVING THEORIES

### Beyond Meteorological and Hoax Theories
As crop circles evolved in complexity, so did the theories about their origins. Researchers began to propose more sophisticated explanations, incorporating advanced scientific principles and technologies.

### Electromagnetic Theories
Some researchers suggested that crop circles might be created by directed electromagnetic waves or microwave energies. These theories posited that such energies could flatten crops in precise patterns, aligning with observed physical changes in the crops, such as blown nodes.

### Extraterrestrial Hypotheses
The idea that crop circles could be messages from extraterrestrial beings gained traction, especially with the increasing complexity and symbolic nature of the formations. Proponents of this theory argued that the patterns could be attempts at communication using universally understood mathematical and geometric principles.

# THE PIONEER PLAQUE
# CONNECTIONS

- 1978-2023 HYDROGEN SIGNATURE
- 2009 SIGNAL DEVICE
- 2014 STAR MAP
- 2002 ALIEN PORTRAIT HOLDING DISC — "WE OPPOSE DECEPTION" — APPEARED OPPOSITE THE BBC WINCHESTER RADIO TRANSMITTER
- 1996-2018 PLANETARY ALIGNMENT SERIES

MOST ABUNDANT ATOM IN THE UNIVERSE

EVERY MESSAGE WE HAVE EVER SENT OUT IN SEARCH OF NON-HUMAN INTELLIGENCE HAS BEEN RESPONDED TO IN CROP FIELD PATTERNS.

WE THINK THERE ARE MANY MORE PATTERNS THAT HAVE NOT YET BEEN DECODED.

FIND OUT MORE ON...

CROP SIGNALS
CROPSIGNALS.APP

# CHAPTER 3: POTENTIAL SIGNALS FROM A HIGHER INTELLIGENCE

Among the thousands of documented crop circle occurrences over the past 40+ years, "The Hydrogen Signature" pattern and the "Arecibo Response" (2001) stand out as particularly compelling. The Hydrogen Signature is significant because it aligns with principles used by SETI, focusing on hydrogen, the most common element in the universe and a potential universally recognisable pattern to denote communication - a greeting symbol. This distinctive pattern has featured regularly in various crop circle patterns, often on its own early in the season or as a base for a more complex design. Similarly, the 2001 Arecibo Response is remarkable for its direct reply to a human-initiated message, exemplifying what we might expect to receive from an extraterrestrial civilization. There are many other reasons that these patterns are significant and this chapter explores these formations in detail, highlighting their potential as evidence of intelligent communication.

## THE HYDROGEN SIGNATURE (1979-2023)

The Hydrogen Signature is one of the most common, significant, and important patterns found in crop circles. It stands as one of the most likely candidates for a sign of highly intelligent communication. This pattern frequently appears both as part of other crop formations and on its own, usually at the beginning of the crop circle season. However, an unusual appearance at the end of the 2023 season further sparked interest and speculation about the meaning of this unusual pattern sequence.

### Historical Context and Early Appearances
One of the earliest and most notable appearances of this pattern was in Wiltshire, England, typically featuring a solid center circle and a single outer circular line, unmistakably a symbol for hydrogen. This symbol has recurred for over 40 years, with the first recorded instance in 1979.

### Significance in Scientific and Extraterrestrial Communication
The importance of hydrogen in scientific and extraterrestrial communication

### THE PIONEER PLAQUE
# CONNECTION

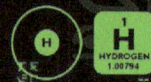

HYDROGEN IS DEPICTED ON THE PIONEER PLAQUE FOR COMMUNICATION WITH OTHER INTELLIGENT LIFEFORMS AS YET UKNOWN TO US. SIMILARLY SETI SCANS THE HYDROGEN FREQUENCY FOR SIGNALS.

**THIS PATTERN APPEARS YEARLY IN CROP FIELDS...**

MOST ABUNDANT ATOM IN THE UNIVERSE

**1978-2023 HYDROGEN DEPICTIONS**

# THE HYDROGEN SIGNATURE

EVERY MESSAGE WE HAVE EVER SENT OUT IN SEARCH OF NON-HUMAN INTELLIGENCE HAS BEEN RESPONDED TO IN CROP FIELD PATTERNS.

WE THINK THERE ARE MANY MORE PATTERNS THAT HAVE NOT YET BEEN DECODED.

FIND OUT MORE ON...

**CROPSIGNALS.APP**

is profound. Hydrogen is the most abundant element in the universe, making it a logical starting point for interstellar communication attempts. Its simplicity and universality mean that any intelligent civilization would likely recognize and understand this symbol.

SETI (Search for Extraterrestrial Intelligence) scans the hydrogen line radio frequency at 1420 MHz, the same frequency emitted by accelerated hydrogen atoms. This frequency is thought to be a universal signal that intelligent beings might use to communicate. The famous "Wow! signal," detected in 1977 at this hydrogen line frequency, was hypothesized to be of alien origin due to its intensity.

Similarly, the Pioneer plaque, attached to the Pioneer 10 and Pioneer 11 spacecraft, portrays the hyperfine transition of neutral hydrogen and uses this wavelength as a standard scale of measurement. This plaque was intended to be universally understandable by any other intelligent species that might encounter the spacecraft, featuring a similar depiction of hydrogen.

**Recurrent Patterns and Their Implications**
The recurrent appearance of the Hydrogen Signature in crop circles suggests a deliberate pattern rather than random occurrences. This repetition indicates that the symbol holds particular significance, potentially as a key to understanding more complex messages embedded within the formations.

The Hydrogen Signature often appears at the beginning of the crop circle season, seemingly announcing a new series of messages. Its unexpected appearance at the end of the 2023 season has led some researchers to speculate about the reasons behind this change, considering it a possible shift in communication strategy or a response to external factors.

**The Hydrogen Line and SETI**
The hydrogen line radio frequency at 1420 MHz is considered a likely candidate for interstellar communication. The rationale is that any technologically advanced civilization would be aware of hydrogen's prominence and might use its frequency to send signals across vast distances. The "Wow! signal" remains a tantalizing clue in the search for intelligent life beyond Earth, detected at this frequency with unexplained intensity.

## The Pioneer Plaque and Universal Symbols

The Pioneer plaque, designed by Carl Sagan and Frank Drake, includes a representation of the hyperfine transition of neutral hydrogen, serving as a universal constant that any intelligent species could recognize and understand. The inclusion of the hydrogen symbol on the Pioneer plaque underscores its importance as a potential means of communication. The similarity between this symbol and those found in crop circles suggests that the creators of these formations might be using a universally recognized element to convey their messages.

# THE ARECIBO RESPONSE (2001)

## The Original Arecibo Message

In 1974, the Arecibo message was broadcast by SETI towards the globular star cluster M13. This binary-coded message contained information about human biology, our solar system, and Earth's technology. It was designed to introduce humanity to potential extraterrestrial civilizations.

## The 2001 Response Formation

In 2001, a crop formation appeared beside the Chilbolton Observatory in Hampshire, UK, that seemed to be a direct response to the Arecibo message. This formation contained several fascinating modifications to the original message, providing insight into the senders' identity and biology:

## Biological Structure

The response indicated the senders were silicon-based rather than carbon-based and possessed an extra strand in their DNA, suggesting a radically different biochemistry.

## Physical Appearance

The senders were depicted as significantly shorter than humans with larger heads, a common depiction in popular culture of extraterrestrial beings.

## Planetary System

The formation suggested they inhabited three out of nine planets, possibly within our solar system or another similar system. The depiction included details resembling our solar system but with notable differences.

# THE ARECIBO MESSAGE RESPONSE

## WE SENT THIS MESSAGE IN 1974
SENT TO CONTACT OTHER INTELLIGENT LIFE

26.7 YEARS LATER IN A CROP PATTERN →

## WE GOT THIS RESPONSE IN 2001
APPEARED OVERNIGHT IN A FIELD OF WHEAT

- OUR **NUMERIC** SYSTEMS **ARE THE SAME**
- WE ARE CARBON BASED — **THEY ARE SILICON BASED**
- OUR **BIOLOGICAL** SYSTEMS **ARE THE SAME**
- WE ARE AROUND 5-6 FT — **THEY ARE 2-3 FT TALL**
- **THEIR DNA HAS AN EXTRA STRAND**
- DEPICTIONS OF THE BEINGS WHO TRANSMITTED THE SIGNALS
- **THEIR POPULATION IS 3-4 TIMES OURS**
- WE INHABIT THE EARTH — **THEY INHABIT THE EARTH, MARS AND SATURN**
- DEPICTIONS OF THE DEVICES USED TO TRANSMIT THE SIGNALS

**20TH AUG 2001**

**SIGNAL RANK: 1** — TOP SIGNAL

**RATING: 9.7/10** — CERTIFIED SIGNAL

APPEARING IN A UK CROP FIELD WAS EXACTLY WHAT WE WOULD EXPECT FROM A NON-HUMAN INTELLIGENCE. A DETAILED RESPONSE TO A MESSAGE BROADCAST OUT TO SPACE IN 1974! FIND OUT MORE ON OUR WEBSITE...

**CROP SIGNALS**
CROPSIGNALS.APP

**THEIR BROADCAST DEVICE** APPEARED IN AUGUST 2000 NEARBY THE YEAR BEFORE...

## Population and Mathematics

The senders used a mathematical system similar to ours and indicated a total population of around 30 billion. The layout of their population depiction might offer clues about the distribution among planets or locations.

## The Signal Transmission Agrogram and the Mysterious Face

In 2000, a year before the Arecibo Response, another crop formation appeared depicting the device used to broadcast the message. This agrogram featured an intricate design resembling advanced technology, suggesting the sender's advanced capabilities.

Additionally, a formation depicting a face, reminiscent of the "Face on Mars," appeared alongside the response agrogram. This formation, possibly a self-portrait of the sender, clearly depicted a face in a format reminiscent of the technique used for photos in newspapers, adding another layer of intrigue to the potential communication.

# POTENTIAL SIGNALS SUMMARY

The Hydrogen Signature and the Arecibo Response stand as compelling pieces of evidence suggesting crop circles could be messages from a higher intelligence. The Hydrogen Signature, with its scientific and universal significance, aligns with what SETI might look for in potential higher intelligence communication. The Arecibo Response exemplifies the kind of direct reply humanity might expect to receive from an extraterrestrial civilization or higher intelligence.

# CHAPTER 4: OTHER NOTABLE MODERN CROP CIRCLE CASES

The Hydrogen Signature and the Arecibo response might be the most likely signals from a higher intelligence seen in crop circles, but there are many other examples that compete for that title. This chapter covers several notable cases, detailing the evidence and providing explainations for why these patterns are good candidates for signals from a higher intelligence.

## THE JULIA SET (1996)

### Overview and Description

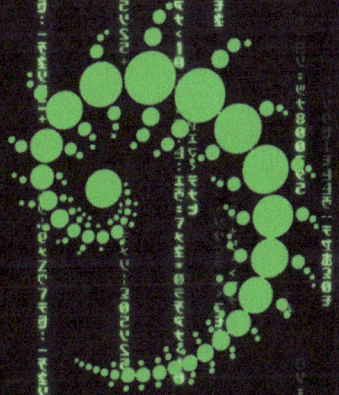

On July 7, 1996, a pilot flying over Stonehenge reported seeing a large, intricate crop circle formation that had not been present just 45 minutes earlier. The formation resembled a variation of the "Julia Set" complex fractal, pattern derived from mathematical equations. Interestingly the pilot later retracted his statement and despite pilots being acutely observant by nature, claimed he could have been "mistaken" in having not observed it during his first flight over the area.

### Details and Impact

The "Julia Set" formation spanned approximately 150 feet in diameter and consisted of 151 circles in total. Its sudden appearance, precise geometry, and mathematical sophistication stunned both researchers and skeptics. This formation significantly challenged the human hoax theory, given the scale, complexity, and rapid creation time.

### Scientific and Public Reaction

The Julia Set drew widespread media coverage and scientific interest. Researchers noted the mathematical precision and speculated on the possibility of advanced technologies or non-human intelligence behind its creation. Public interest in the formation contributed to a major surge in crop circle tourism and further investigations.

# THE MILK HILL GALAXY SPIRAL (2001)

## Overview and Description
In August 2001, a spectacular crop circle formation appeared at Milk Hill in Wiltshire, England. This formation, known as the "Milk Hill Galaxy Spiral" consisted of over 400 individual circles arranged in a spiral pattern spanning approximately 700 feet in diameter, one of the largest and most complex designs to ever appear and it appeared overnight in 6 hours during heavy rainfall, with no trace of any muddy footprints over the flattened crop.

## Details and Complexity
The Galaxy Spiral pattern's sheer size and complexity were unprecedented. Researchers marveled at the precision and scale, noting that such a formation would be extremely challenging to create overnight without advanced planning and tools.

## Public and Scientific Reaction
The formation received extensive media attention and became a focal point for crop circle researchers. It's complexity and scale bolstered arguments against the hoax theory and fueled speculation about non-human origins.

# THE CRABWOOD ALIEN PORTRAIT (2002)

## Description and Location
On August 15, 2002, an extraordinary crop circle formation appeared in a field near Crabwood, Hampshire, UK. The formation was situated next to the BBC Winchester radio transmitter, which adds an intriguing layer of context to its appearance. The crop circle depicted a striking portrait of a humanoid face resembling the stereotypical "Grey" alien, complete with large, almond-shaped eyes. In the alien's hand was a circular disc featuring a binary code message. Above the alien's right shoulder, the formation included what appears to be the three stars of Orion's Belt.

## Message Decoding
The binary code on the disc, when decoded using ASCII, revealed the message:

# "BEWARE THE BEARERS OF FALSE GIFTS & THEIR BROKEN PROMISES. MUCH PAIN BUT STILL TIME. BELIEVE. THERE IS GOOD OUT THERE. WE OPPOSE DECEPTION. CONDUIT CLOSING."

The message, with its direct warning and cryptic tone, stands out for its combination of visual artistry and textual content. This detailed depiction and its ominous message intrigued both researchers and the public, adding significant weight to the ongoing debate about the origins and purposes of crop circles.

## Significance and Impact
The "Crabwood Alien Portrait" formation made headlines due to its precise and elaborate design, which appeared alongside the BBC Winchester radio

APPEARED IN **2002** FOLLOWING A **2001** BBC REPORT WHERE THE REPORTER ANNOUNCED THE COLLAPSE OF WTC BUILDING 7...
**...20 MINUTES BEFORE IT ACTUALLY COLLAPSED!**

APPEARED IN A CROP FIELD JUST OPPOSITE THE BBC WINCHESTER RADIO TRANSMITTER...

"BEWARE THE BEARERS OF FALSE GIFTS AND THEIR BROKEN PROMISES. MUCH PAIN BUT STILL TIME. BELIEVE. THERE IS GOOD OUT THERE. WE OPPOSE DECEPTION. CONDUIT CLOSING."

"WE OPPOSE DECEPTION"

THE 3 STARS OF ORION'S BELT?

# THE ALIEN PORTRAIT

PORTRAIT PHOTO STYLE RENDITION OF A GREY ALIEN CLEARLY DEPICTED HOLDING AN ASCII ENCODED DISC WITH A CLEAR MESSAGE IN ENGLISH. WAS THIS A DIRECT RESPONSE TO THE POWERS THAT BE AS WELL AS A MESSAGE TO ALL OF HUMANITY?

EVERY MESSAGE WE HAVE EVER SENT OUT IN SEARCH OF NON-HUMAN INTELLIGENCE HAS BEEN RESPONDED TO IN CROP FIELD PATTERNS.

WE THINK THERE ARE MANY MORE PATTERNS THAT HAVE NOT YET BEEN DECODED.

FIND OUT MORE ON...

**CROP SIGNALS**

CROPSIGNALS.APP

transmitter. Its similarity in location to the Arecibo response binary strip formation, which appeared near the Chilbolton Observatory just over a year earlier, is notable. The dimensions of the Crabwood formation—59 meters by 33 meters—when multiplied, total 1947, a number linked to the Roswell incident, adding another layer of intrigue.

There have been claims that the Crabwood formation was a commissioned hoax, possibly as a marketing stunt for the film "Signs," which was released on August 2, 2002, just 13 days before the crop circle's appearance. However, if this was indeed a marketing stunt, it is surprising that no legal actions were taken against those responsible for creating such a prominent and controversial message in a private field directly next to the BBC Winchester

tower. The elaborate nature of the formation and its politically charged message suggest it might have been more than a mere promotional gimmick.

Considering the complex design and its placement near a major broadcasting station, it's plausible that this crop circle was either a highly elaborate statement from human pranksters or a direct message to humanity. The possibility that it was a political statement or a response to the reporting surrounding the collapse of a certain building the previous year cannot be dismissed. Alternatively, it might represent an attempt to communicate something of significant importance to authorities or the public at large. The precise and deliberate nature of the Crabwood formation continues to fuel speculation about its true origin and intent.

## THE CYMATIC SERIES (2001)

### Overview & Description
The Cymatic series refers to a set of crop formations that appeared in 2001, resembling cymatic patterns—geometric shapes created by sound vibrations on a surface. These formations provide a fascinating connection between crop circles and the concept of sound as a medium for communication.

### Key Formation
One notable formation from this series depicted an octahedral cymatic pattern composed of eight 5-pointed stars. Appearing in the same year as the Arecibo response, this pattern fits the profile of a universal symbol that might be used by a higher intelligence to communicate or convey intelligence with other beings in the universe.

### Implications
The Cymatic series suggests that the creators of these crop circles might be using sound or vibration as a means of communication. This aligns with theories proposing that crop circles could be the result of advanced technology or a higher intelligence utilizing natural principles to convey intelligence and establish contact.

# THE DNA DISC (2002)

## Overview and Description

In late 2002, near Boomerang Stables in Crooked Soley, Berkshire, an extraordinary crop circle appeared, dubbed the "DNA Disc". This formation, measuring between 300-400 feet in diameter, depicted a DNA spiral divided into six sections, arranged in the style of binary bits on a disc. It emerged in a wheat field close to harvest, captivating researchers and enthusiasts alike.

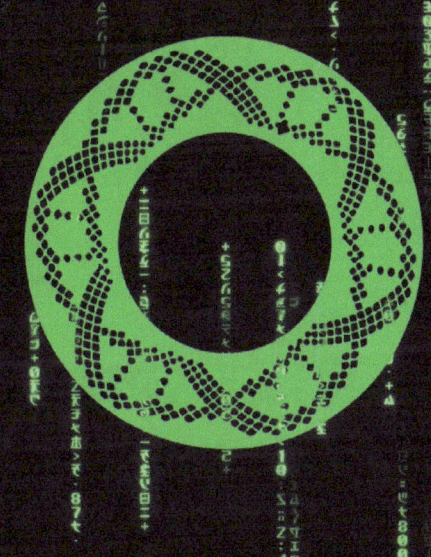

## Details and Impact

The DNA Disc's timing, at the end of the crop circle season, added to its mystique. Its design clearly represented DNA as information or data, sparking debates about its origins and purpose. The formation's binary representation suggested a profound understanding of genetic coding. Also noteworthy could be fact that the DNA loops around the sections of 6 and the sheer precision and complexity of the pattern.

## Scientific Context and Implications

The concept of using DNA for information storage was theorized in 1959, and experiments began in 1988. However, binary encoding in DNA storage was only successfully implemented in 2007, five years after the DNA Disc's appearance. This raises intriguing questions about the formation's origins. Could it have been a prescient indication of future scientific advancements, or was it an incredibly sophisticated hoax?

## The 2002 Connection

The DNA Disc appeared in the same year as the Alien Portrait holding a binary disc, suggesting a thematic link between the two formations. This coincidence hints at an intent to convey complex information about genetics and data storage in this pair of designs that were clearly intended to mimic our level of technology at the time and demonstrating the intelligence behind it is watching the progression of humanity very closely.

# BORYEONG DNA (2008)

This formation, appearing in a South Korean rice field early in the crop season, featured two clear indicators of nucleotides with an outer circle intersected by three smaller circles. The meaning of the smaller circles remains unclear, though some other researchers have suggested these represent planetary or solar movement.

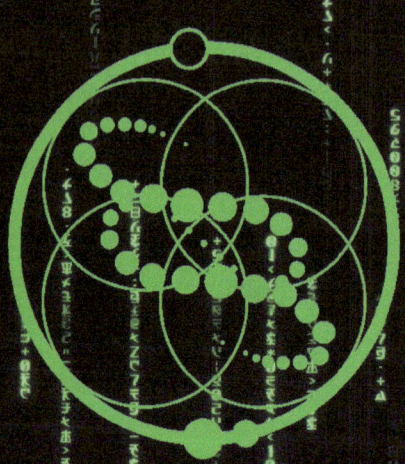

The "Boryeong DNA" formation is particularly intriguing because the inner four circles could not have been made using the conventional rope and board method, as the crop remains undisturbed in the center of each circle. Additionally, there were no signs of field entry or tractor tramlines, raising questions about its construction. Visitors to the Boryeong circle reported a strange electrical energy, a common occurrence in many crop circle sites.

### Significance and Public Reaction
The DNA Disc garnered significant media and scholarly interest. Its precise and complex design challenged hoax theories, prompting many to consider the possibility of non-human involvement. The formation's suggestion of DNA as an information storage medium aligned with cutting-edge scientific research, further fueling speculation about its origins.

### DNA Related Formations Summary
The DNA Disc stands as a remarkable example of the intersection between crop circle phenomena and advanced scientific concepts. Its detailed representation of DNA and binary encoding, appearing years before such technology became a reality, suggests a level of sophistication that is difficult to attribute solely to human pranksters. Whether these formations are products of extraordinary foresight or genuine signals from a higher intelligence, they remain a fascinating subject for ongoing investigation.

# THE ROSWELL ROCK FORMATION (1996)

**Discovery and Description**
This formation appeared to depict cycles of an eclipse sequence. Intriguingly, eight years after the appearance of this crop circle, a rock was found inscribed with the exact same pattern not far from Roswell, New Mexico, USA. The origins and means of construction of the rock are unknown and cannot be verified beyond doubt, but it is believed by some to be a relic from the 1947 Roswell incident. Scientific study of the rock has so far been inconclusive and researchers are still unclear on the true nature of the rock.

**Significance and Theories**
The similarities between the Roswell Rock's pattern and this 1996 crop circle pattern have led to speculation about their connection. Some researchers believe the rock might be a UFO part or a form of communication or marker left by extraterrestrial visitors. The precise design match suggests a link between the crop circles and the Roswell incident, potentially pointing to a broader narrative of extraterrestrial interaction with Earth. Skeptics claim the rock is a sophisticated prank that was created to give credence to the idea of crop circles being of otherworldly origin.

**THIS ROCK WAS FOUND NEAR ROSWELL, NEW MEXICO IN 2004**

# THE BLUEPRINT SERIES (2008)

## Overview and Description

In 2008, a series of crop circles appeared that captivated researchers with their striking resemblance to technical blueprints. Among these patterns were depictions that seemed to illustrate complex mechanical devices. One formation resembled a rotational cut section, while another included a spiral cut section that appeared to be a blueprint or an applicator of some kind. These formations have been collectively referred to as the "Blueprint Series."

## Details and Theories

The Blueprint Series drew significant attention due to its intricate designs that suggested a 2D representation of a 3D object. Some theorists proposed that these patterns could be blueprints for constructing advanced technology, possibly even an anti-gravity device. The precise nature of the designs, which included detailed and symmetrical elements, hinted at a level of sophistication beyond typical human hoaxing.

## Attempts at Construction

Intrigued by the possibility that the Blueprint Series could represent a functional device, some researchers and engineers attempted to construct the depicted object. While at least one known attempt failed, it remains unclear whether subsequent efforts led to any substantive outcomes. The complexity and technical detail of the designs suggest that, if genuine, they could represent advanced technology not yet understood by science.

## Significance and Impact

The appearance of the Blueprint Series in 2008 marked a notable shift in crop circle phenomena. These patterns were not merely symbolic or artistic but seemed to convey specific technical information. The suggestion that these blueprints could be instructions for building a device added a new dimension to the study of crop circles, blurring the lines between art, science, and potential extraterrestrial communication.

### Follow-Up? The 2009 Device Depiction
In 2009, a year after the Blueprint Series, another intriguing formation appeared. This crop circle depicted what looked like a device broadcasting an alien language. The detailed pattern suggested a machine or apparatus, further supporting the idea that the crop circles could be transmitting technical knowledge or instructions.

### Context and Interpretation
The Blueprint Series and the subsequent 2009 device depiction raised important questions about the purpose and origins of crop circles. If these formations were indeed blueprints or technical schematics, they could represent an attempt by a higher intelligence to communicate complex information to humanity. The designs' technical nature and the timing of their appearances suggest a deliberate effort to convey knowledge that could be crucial for technological advancement.

The Blueprint Series of 2008, followed by the device depiction in 2009, underscores the potential for crop circles to serve as more than mere artistic expressions. These formations hint at a deeper purpose, possibly conveying advanced technological knowledge. Whether these patterns are genuine messages from a higher intelligence or elaborate human creations, they continue to intrigue and inspire those who study the crop circle phenomenon. The possibility that these designs could lead to significant technological breakthroughs remains an exciting prospect for future research.

## POTENTIAL SIGNAL DEVICE DEPICTIONS

## THE 2000 SIGNAL DEVICE FORMATION

### Overview and Description
In the year 2000, a notable crop circle appeared that seemed to depict a broadcast device remarkably similar to the one later shown in the Arecibo Message response. This formation appeared almost exactly one year before the Arecibo Response formation, which depicted an update to the original Arecibo message by replacing the human broadcast device with a new, unknown device.

### Details and Theories
The 2000 formation appeared to depict a chain reaction or a mechanism involving some form of energy transmission, possibly microwave energy, which many theorists believe is involved in the flattening of the crops. The intricate design suggested a sophisticated technology that could potentially be used for communication or transmission of signals.

### Connection to the Arecibo Response
When the Arecibo Response appeared in 2001, it featured a similar device in the place of the original human signal transmitter depicted in the 1974 Arecibo message. This connection between the 2000 crop circle and the Arecibo Response strengthened the theory that the formations might be depicting advanced technological devices for communication.

### Significance and Impact
The 2000 signal device formation marked an important development in the study of crop circles. Its detailed and technical design hinted at the possibility of advanced technology being depicted through these patterns. This formation, along with the Arecibo Response, suggested a deliberate attempt to communicate or share advanced knowledge with humanity.

# THE 2009 DEVICE DEPICTION

**Overview and Description**
In 2009, another significant crop circle formation appeared, seemingly depicting the transmission of an alien language or pattern. This formation unfolded in three stages over the course of just over a week and appeared to show a device projecting a strange language or pattern.

**Details and Theories**
The first two parts of the 2009 formation depicted a device, while the third part showed a series of patterns that appeared to be a language or communication method. Some theorists believe this formation could be illustrating the mechanism used for creating crop circles. Others suggest it might be a more detailed or cross-sectional view of the known transmission device depicted in the Arecibo Response.

**Potential Mechanism for Crop Circle Creation**
The detailed depiction of the device in the 2009 formation provided insights into the potential technology behind crop circle creation. The progressive stages seemed to illustrate a process of signal transmission, possibly using energy or technology unknown to contemporary science.

**Significance and Impact**
The 2009 signal device depiction added another layer of complexity to the crop circle phenomenon. By illustrating a potential method for creating crop circles or transmitting signals, this formation provided valuable clues about the technology and intent behind these enigmatic patterns. The intricate design and the staged progression of the formation suggested a sophisticated and deliberate attempt to communicate with humanity.

The signal device depictions in 2000 and 2009 highlight the potential for crop circles to represent advanced technological concepts. These formations suggest a method of communication or signal transmission that could be linked to the creation of crop circles themselves. Whether these patterns are genuine messages from a higher intelligence or elaborate human constructions, they continue to intrigue researchers and inspire ongoing investigations into the mysteries of crop circles.

**STAGE 1**
21 JUNE 2009

**STAGE 3**
28 JUNE 2009

**STAGE 2**
22 JUNE 2009

# SIGNAL TRANSMITTER

# CROP SIGNALS

COULD THIS DEPICT STAGE 4?
A WHIRLWIND OF LIGHT ORBS
& "THE CARBON SIGNATURE"
KNOLL DOWN, WILTSHIRE, UK
**JUNE 2009**

# CHAPTER 5: LOCATION ANOMALIES OF CROP CIRCLES

The geographical distribution of crop circles offers intriguing insights into their potential origins and purpose. A significant majority of the most compelling crop circles appear within a specific region in the UK, particularly within a 50-mile radius of Stonehenge. This chapter explores the notable characteristics of these locations and the theories surrounding their significance.

## PROXIMITY TO ANCIENT SITES

**Stonehenge and Surrounding Area**
A remarkable 90% of the most likely genuine crop circles have been documented within 50 miles of Stonehenge. This proximity to one of the world's most famous ancient sites suggests a deliberate choice of location, possibly to enhance visibility and significance. Stonehenge itself is a prehistoric monument with astronomical alignments, hinting at an advanced understanding of celestial events by its builders. The frequent appearance of crop circles in this area may imply a connection to ancient knowledge or an effort to draw attention to these historical sites.

**Other Ancient Structures**
Crop circles also commonly appear near other ancient structures, such as stone circles, barrows, and suspected artificial hills. These locations have long been considered sacred or significant in various cultures, and their association with crop circles adds another layer of mystery. Some theorize that these sites might have been chosen due to their historical and cultural importance, potentially serving as markers or beacons for communication from higher intelligences.

## THE CHALK WHITE HORSES CONNECTION

**Historical and Cultural Significance**
The phenomenon of crop circles has a notable correlation with the Chalk White Horses of the UK. These iconic hill figures, carved into the British

countryside, add another layer of mystery to the crop circle enigma. The UK is home to 16 known Chalk White Horses, primarily located in Wiltshire, Hampshire, and Oxfordshire. These figures are part of the rich tapestry of megalithic structures in this region, which also includes Stonehenge and Avebury.

## POSSIBLE THEORIES

### Targeted Contact Due to Historical Significance

One theory posits that the UK, with its historical significance as a global power, might have been a prime target for contact by higher intelligences. During the height of the British Empire, the UK was a focal point of global influence and innovation. Crop circles appearing near these historically significant sites could be seen as a strategic choice to ensure maximum visibility and impact.

### Ancient Astronomical Markers and Energy Lines

Another theory suggests that the Chalk White Horses, along with other megalithic structures, are positioned along ancient ley lines—energy paths that crisscross the Earth. These ley lines are believed to hold significant spiritual and magnetic properties. Crop circles might be tapping into these energy lines, utilizing the Earth's natural energies to create their formations.

### Genetic Manipulation and the Gift of the Horse

A more speculative theory involves the genetic origins of horses themselves. Some researchers propose that horses, much like humans, exhibit signs of genetic manipulation. This theory posits that horses were engineered as a gift to humanity from a higher intelligence. The proximity of crop circles to the Chalk White Horses might symbolize a connection to this ancient gift, serving as a reminder of humanity's intertwined destinies with these majestic animals.

## POTENTIAL TECHNOLOGIC OR NATURAL CAUSES

### Underground Aquifers

One theory suggests that the technology behind genuine crop circles may rely on underground aquifers. These natural reservoirs of water could play a role in the formation of crop circles, possibly acting as conduits for energy or as part of a larger technological system. The interaction between underground water systems and the land above could create conditions conducive to the appearance of crop circles, especially in areas rich in aquifers.

### Advanced Buried Technology?

Another speculative idea is that there may be advanced technology buried beneath the surface in these areas. This technology could function similarly to how radar dishes reflect signals, using the Earth's surface to transmit crop circle patterns. The precise and intricate designs of many crop circles suggest a level of sophistication that might be explained by hidden technology, potentially involving quantum entanglement to transmit information across vast distances instantaneously.

## GOLDEN BALL HILL & SURROUNDING AREAS

### Golden Ball Hill

Golden Ball Hill, a site of frequent crop circle activity, reportedly gets its name from the presence of the light orb phenomena. This location in Wiltshire has been home to some of the most famous crop circle patterns. The association with light orbs adds an intriguing dimension to the mystery, suggesting a possible link between the phenomena of crop circles and unexplained aerial lights.

### Sugar Hill and Milk Hill

Oddly named Sugar Hill and Milk Hill are also sites of frequent profound crop circle designs. Both locations are within the same area of Wiltshire, contributing to the cluster of crop circle activity in this region. The consistent appearance of complex and noteworthy patterns at these sites highlights the significance of this area in the broader crop circle phenomena.

## DISTRIBUTION & DESIGN ANOMALIES

### Mismatch with Graffiti Patterns

The distribution and design of crop circles do not align with what we would expect if they were purely man-made phenomena. Unlike graffiti for example, which typically appears in urban areas and follows patterns of accessibility and visibility, crop circles often appear in rural and sometimes remote locations. They are frequently found near ancient sites and other culturally significant landmarks, rather than in places where human artists are most likely to operate.

**Random Global Occurrences**
Even more puzzling is the fact that perfect crop circles seem to randomly appear all over the world. This would not be expected if they were the work of highly specialized human artists, who would likely operate within specific regions or follow particular trends. The random yet precise nature of these formations suggests the involvement of unknown factors or advanced technologies.

## LOCATION ANOMALIES SUMMARY

The geographical anomalies and specific locations of crop circles offer compelling clues about their origins and purpose. The consistent appearance of crop circles near ancient sites, within a specific region, and in proximity to the Chalk White Horses suggests a deliberate and meaningful choice of locations. Whether influenced by natural energies, advanced technology, or historical significance, these locations continue to be a focal point for those seeking to understand the phenomenon of crop circles. As we explore these geographical patterns, we move closer to unraveling the complex relationship between crop circles and the ancient and modern landscapes they adorn.

# CHAPTER 6: HUMAN-MADE HOAXES & A POTENTIAL COVER UP OPERATION

While many believe all crop circles are created by unknown or extraterrestrial forces, a small percentage of occurrences have been proven to be human-made hoaxes. This chapter documents some known hoaxes, acknowledges the skill and effort required to create complex designs, and examines the limitations of the man-made hypothesis. It also addresses the actions of individuals within the crop circle community who promote the idea that all crop circles are man-made and the potential for this to be a part of a broader disinformation campaign.

## DOCUMENTATION OF KNOWN HOAXES

### Doug Bower and Dave Chorley: The Birth of Modern Hoaxes

In the late 1980s, Doug Bower and Dave Chorley, two British pranksters, claimed responsibility for many early crop circles. Using planks, ropes, and simple tools, they demonstrated their technique for creating crop circles. Their admission and demonstrations led to widespread belief that many crop circles were human-made hoaxes.

### Impact on Public Perception

Bower and Chorley's claims significantly impacted public perception, leading many to dismiss crop circles as mere pranks. Their work inspired other hoaxers worldwide, contributing to a proliferation of man-made crop circles. Their admission was extensively covered by the media, reinforcing the narrative that crop circles were the result of elaborate pranks rather than unexplained phenomena.

## OTHER NOTABLE HOAXERS

### Circlemakers Collective

Following Bower and Chorley's revelations, various groups and individuals claim to have taken up circle making as an art form.

**B1ackprojects**
Based in the UK, became well-known for their intricate designs, often created for commercial purposes, including advertisements and promotional events.

**Public Demonstrations:** Several public demonstrations by artists and hoaxers have shown that moderately complex crop circles can be created by humans. These demonstrations typically involve teams working overnight using planks, ropes, and surveying tools to ensure precision and symmetry.

## KNOWN CASES OF HUMAN-MADE HOAXES

**Mothership Glass (Antsy), 2016:** Apparently commissioned as a marketing stunt by a U.S. based company, this crop circle featured hieroglyphics in place of the letters spelling "MOTHERSHIP" the name of the brand. Created over several days and well documented with photographic evidence, it is one of the most complex human-made formations and fooled many into believing it was of alien origin before the hoax was revealed. Notably, the messy lay of this formation contrasts with the cleaner lays of many crop circles that are of unknown origin.

**Barbers Razor, 2023:** A depiction of a razor appeared in a crop circle, fooling many believers in alien origins into thinking it could be a signal that the world might end. Several days later however, a video surfaced showing its creation, apparently it was a commission for a barber shop logo. Some still believe this and other formations are cover-ups or asserting that making a crop circle as complicated as Antsy is impossible, despite evidence to the contrary.

**Cymatic 7-Fold Star, 2024:** A cymatic star formation closely matched a detailed drawing posted several months prior by crop circle artist Dan Davies aka. "Cropsy". Notably, this was the only pattern in 2024 with multiple points of evidence supporting it as man-made: it featured an imperfect lay and was predicted by a known crop circle artist. This highlights the potential for human artistry to replicate intricate patterns that some might attribute to unknown or extraterrestrial forces, but also strange that this was the only pattern out of all of them that anyone was able to predict. As several predictions were made by Dan, this similarity could have been by chance.

## LAND ARTISTS: DENE HINE & FRANCESCO GRASSI

**Dene Hine** claims to have made hundreds of crop circles in the UK under the banner of "Team Clandestine". While he has produced comparatively little evidence to support this, he has proven to be capable of creating crop circles and has reportedly contributed to both the Antsy and the Razor formations.

**Francesco Grassi** has claimed responsibility for many crop circles in Italy and has provided evidence supporting creation of several notable formations.

While there does appear to be some evidence supporting that they have indeed made several complex formations, they both also seem to have made it their mission to eliminate any notion of mystery surrounding the phenomena. Both have made the claim that all crop circles are man made and seem to be compelled to use their authority to push that narrative. Many who oppose this hypothesis suggest that these gentlemen and others could be part of a continuation of the same "Doug and Dave" disinformation campaign, to cover up the true origins of crop circles

## THE SKILL & EFFORT REQUIRED FOR COMPLEX DESIGN EXECUTION

### Planning and Design
Creating a complex crop circle requires meticulous planning, detailed blueprints and effective communication. Designers may use computer software to create precise geometric patterns and calculate measurements before heading into the field. Larger and more intricate crop circles require coordinated efforts from multiple individuals, working efficiently and silently, often under the cover of darkness, to complete their designs before dawn.

### Execution
Hoaxers use various tools, including planks, ropes, and surveying equipment. They carefully flatten the crops without breaking the stems, a technique known as "stomping". The time and effort required to create a complex crop circle can be substantial, demanding not only physical effort but also a high degree of skill and precision.

# THE MAN-MADE HYPOTHESIS & ITS LIMITATIONS

## Frequency and Complexity of Crop Circles

As crop circles have evolved, their complexity has increased dramatically. The intricate geometric shapes, fractals, and mathematically significant patterns observed in many crop circles challenge the capabilities of even the most skilled hoaxers.

The sheer number of crop circles reported each year, particularly during peak seasons, raises questions about the feasibility of them all being human-made. The time, effort, and resources required to produce such a large volume of formations are considerable.

# LOGISTICAL CHALLENGES

## Scale and Location

Some crop circles are enormous in scale, spanning hundreds of meters in diameter. Creating such large formations, especially in remote or heavily monitored locations, presents significant logistical challenges for human hoaxers.

## Overnight Appearances

Many crop circles appear overnight, often in fields adjacent to busy roads or under constant surveillance. The ability to create complex designs in such a short timeframe without being detected further complicates the man-made hypothesis.

# THE AGENDA OF CERTAIN INDIVIDUALS

## The Gaslighting Campaigns

Some individuals within the crop circle community have taken a controversial approach by suggesting that because some crop circles have been proven to be man-made, that means all crop circles must be man-made. This is known as the man made narrative and clearly gaslighting at its finest. This narrative is often accompanied by attempts to discredit historical accounts and documented instances of crop circles predating the modern hoax era.

### Historical Revisionism
These individuals frequently attempt to undermine written history, such as the "Mowing Devil" incident from the 17th century. By discrediting historical evidence, they aim to reinforce the idea that crop circles are a recent phenomenon created by modern hoaxers. This approach serves to discredit any evidence that does not align with their narrative.

## PATTERNS OF DISINFORMATION

### Uniform Agenda
Many of those pushing this narrative share common agendas, often linked to personal gain or the promotion of specific theories. Their efforts frequently involve selective presentation of evidence and the dismissal of counterarguments. This pattern of behavior raises questions about the possibility of a coordinated disinformation campaign.

### Continuation of the Doug and Dave Explanation
The aggressive promotion of the man-made hypothesis and the discrediting of historical evidence resemble a continuation of the Doug and Dave debacle. Just as Bower and Chorley's revelations were used to dismiss all crop circles, the current narrative attempts to cover up or explain away any evidence that challenges the simplistic man-made explanation.

## PROPAGATION OF THE DOUG & DAVE STORY

### Story Impact
The narrative that Doug Bower and Dave Chorley were responsible for most crop circles became widely accepted, especially after their public demonstrations and being present at the location of several early formations. This story was used to explain away the growing number of complex and large formations that appeared. By attributing all crop circles to a few individuals, it created a convenient, if simplistic, solution to a complex phenomenon in the minds of many.

## Media Amplification

The media played a significant role in amplifying the Doug and Dave origin explanation. Their story was sensationalized and presented as a definitive answer to the crop circle mystery. This widespread media coverage contributed to the belief that human hoaxers were behind all crop circles, overshadowing other potential explanations.

## Challenges to the Story

Despite the widespread belief in the Doug and Dave explanation, numerous attempts to replicate even simple crop circle patterns have failed. Researchers and amateur enthusiasts alike have struggled to recreate complex designs, especially those featuring intricate geometric and fractal patterns.

# HUMAN-MADE HOAXES SUMMARY

While human-made hoaxes account for a small number of crop circles, the increasing complexity, volume, and logistical challenges of many formations cast doubt on the man-made hypothesis as a comprehensive explanation. The intricate designs and rapid appearances of some crop circles suggest the involvement of factors beyond simple pranks. The propagation of the Doug and Dave explanation, coupled with attempts to discredit historical evidence and the complexity of replicating certain patterns, suggests broader motives behind promoting the man-made hypothesis. Patterns of disinformation and historical revisionism observed among certain individuals raise concerns about potential cover-up operations and the suppression of evidence that does not fit the man-made narrative. As the investigation into crop circles continues, it is essential to consider all possibilities and remain open to alternative explanations.

# CHAPTER 7: INTERESTING NOVEL THEORIES & CONCEPTS

The crop circle phenomena has inspired a multitude of theories about their origins and meanings. This chapter explores various theories and concepts that have emerged, ranging from scientific hypotheses to wild speculative ideas. We will examine the strengths and weaknesses for each theory, considering the evidence that supports or refutes them.

## NATURAL PHENOMENA THEORIES

### Plasma Vortex Theory
One scientific theory suggests that plasma vortices—tornado-like columns of ionized gas—could be responsible for creating crop circles. Proponents argue that these vortices could flatten crops in specific patterns as they move across fields. However, while plasma vortexes can create circular patterns, the complexity and precision of many crop circles exceed what would be expected from this phenomenon alone.

### Whirlwind and Microburst Theories
Another theory posits that whirlwinds or microbursts, localized downdrafts of wind, could create crop circles. These natural phenomena can cause sudden, intense wind patterns that might flatten crops in circular shapes. While this theory accounts for some simple crop circles, it struggles to explain the intricate designs and large-scale formations observed in more recent years.

## MATHEMATICAL & GEOMETRIC THEORIES

### Fractal Patterns
Many crop circles feature fractal patterns, which are intricate structures that repeat at various scales. Fractals, such as the Julia Set and Mandelbrot Set, exhibit self-similarity and complex geometry. The appearance of these patterns in crop circles suggests an advanced understanding of mathematics and geometry, raising questions about the source of such knowledge.

### Geometric Precision

Crop circles often display geometric precision, including complex shapes like the geometric Pi representation and Euler's identity binary disc. The accuracy of these designs suggests a level of mathematical understanding that goes beyond what would be expected from random natural phenomena or simple human hoaxes.

## EXTRATERRESTRIAL ORIGINS

### Communication Hypotheses

One of the most popular speculative theories is that crop circles are messages from extraterrestrial beings. Proponents argue that the complexity and precision of the designs indicate an advanced intelligence attempting to communicate with humanity. This theory is supported by the idea that radio waves and other forms of communication might be impractical due to interference or detection issues. Instead, crop circles offer a non-intrusive method of conveying messages through visual means.

### Evidence from Arecibo Message and Roswell Connections

The response to the Arecibo message and the Roswell rock formation have been interpreted by some as evidence of extraterrestrial involvement in crop circles. The connection between these events and the appearance of crop circles with similar themes adds weight to the hypothesis of an advanced intelligence attempting to communicate through these formations.

## HISTORICAL & ANCIENT CONNECTIONS

### Sacred Geometry

Sacred geometry encompasses geometric shapes and patterns considered to have spiritual significance, appears frequently in crop circles. Designs such as the Seed of Life and Flower of Life are examples of sacred geometry that have been linked to ancient cultures. The recurrence of these patterns raises questions about whether crop circles might be drawing on historical or ancient knowledge.

## Ancient Astronomical Alignments

Some crop circles appear within a a few miles of Stonehenge and the white horses of Wiltshire, UK. The alignment with these historical landmarks suggests that the creators of these patterns might have some kind of connection to the landmarks. This connection invites speculation about whether crop circles are related to ancient history.

# THE CARBON SIGNATURE

One of the most common Agrograms is the 4-fold circle formation, also known as the quintuplet. Not only does it frequently appear at the beginning of the crop circle season, but it was also among the first recorded crop circle patterns from the late 1970s. Interestingly, it was also one of the first patterns to appear in the new millennium. This design, which contains an inner circle with four outer orbiting circles, has evolved in hundreds of different styles over the years.

## Significance and Interpretations

The quintuplet design is thought to represent one or both of these concepts:
<u>Carbon-Based Life Signature</u> (Methane, $CH_4$): The structure of one central circle surrounded by four others resembles the molecular structure of methane ($CH_4$), a fundamental component of carbon-based life.
Cartesian Coordinate System: The formation might symbolize the Cartesian coordinate system or 2D directionality (north, south, east, west), indicating an understanding of basic spatial orientation.

## DNA and Life

The pattern could also represent the four nucleotides that make up DNA, signifying the building blocks of life. Additionally, it might symbolize the four inner planets of our solar system with the sun at the center.

The dimensionality aspect of the design also seems crucial. It has been observed that natural Agrograms often use 3-fold designs to depict mushrooms, trees, plants, or other static earthbound beings, as well as seed-themed designs. This repetition could indicate a level of consciousness or the basis of life. The majority of animal species Agrograms feature 4 circles in some way, such as the Dragonfly and Hummingbird Agrograms, suggesting a

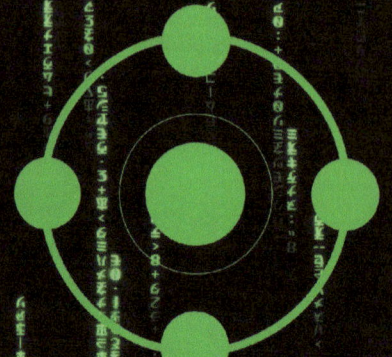

**A FREQUENTLY REPEATING DESIGN THE BASIC CARBON SIGNATURE PATTERN**

**COULD THIS DEPICT A LIGHT ORB WHIRLWIND?
KNOLL DOWN, WILTSHIRE, UK
JUNE 2009**

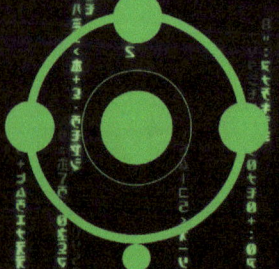

**FIRST UK CROP CIRCLE IN 2024
WILTON WINDMILL, WILTSHIRE, UK
JUNE 2024**

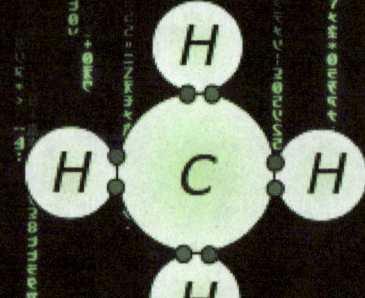

**$CH^4$
METHANE MOLECULE
THE SIGNATURE OF
CARBON BASED LIFE**

connection to CH4 methane, the inner 4 planets around the sun, dimensional mobility or something else entirely.

Others have suggested that 6-fold designs or Sacred Geometry could symbolize consciousness above our own or advanced intelligent life forms, possibly indicating the lifeforms ability to move in three dimensions, as with birds for example. Similarly, 8-fold patterns might symbolize anti-gravity or beings with access to four or more dimensions, an interesting theory.

**Astrobiological Perspective**
Astrophysicists scan exoplanets for biosignatures—chemical signatures produced by life forms and compositions of exoplanet atmospheres—by analyzing light from distant worlds. One of the key elements they look for is depicted in this common crop circle pattern. Interestingly, the same configuration could apply to hypothetical silicon-based life, suggesting this formation may be a universal signature of life in general. Could this be a greeting from a silicon-based or other form of life to us carbon-based beings?

**Plausibility and Skepticism**
As this is a relatively simple design to hoax, it could be argued that its prevalence is due to its ease of creation. However, this does not explain why it predominantly appears early in the season, hinting at its role as a greeting or signal of some kind. The recurrence of the carbon signature in crop circles raises intriguing questions about its origin and purpose, suggesting a deliberate attempt at communication rather than mere coincidence or prank.

In summary, the carbon signature stands as a potent symbol recurring within the crop circle phenomenon, representing fundamental aspects of life, dimensionality, and potentially serving as a universal greeting from one form of life to another. Its simplicity, frequency, and timing in appearance strongly hint at a deeper significance that aligns with the broader patterns observed in crop circles, reinforcing the idea of intelligent design behind these formations.

# THE ROLE OF ADVANCED TECHNOLOGY

### The Need for Advanced Technology
Creating precise and intricate crop circles requires advanced technology and technical expertise. The ability to execute complex designs with high accuracy suggests that the creators might possess technological capabilities beyond those available to the general public. This need for advanced technology supports the hypothesis that crop circles may be the result of an external intelligence or highly skilled practitioners.

### Examples of Technological Precision
Certain crop circles exhibit such precise geometric patterns and alignments that replicating them with basic tools and human effort becomes highly improbable. The use of sophisticated tools or techniques, whether extraterrestrial or otherwise, may be necessary to achieve the level of detail observed in these formations.

# INTERESTING THEORIES & CONCEPTS SUMMARY

Theories and concepts surrounding crop circles are diverse and multifaceted, ranging from scientific explanations to speculative ideas. While natural phenomena and mathematical theories offer valuable insights, they often fall short of explaining the full range of observed crop circle patterns. Speculative theories, including extraterrestrial involvement and ancient connections, provide intriguing possibilities but lack definitive evidence. The recurring symbols and advanced technology required to create some crop circles further complicate the narrative. As research continues, it is essential to consider all theories and remain open to new evidence that may shed light on the true origins and meanings of crop circles.

# CHAPTER 8: MATHEMATICS & GEOMETRY

Crop circles have fascinated observers for decades with the complex mathematical and geometric patterns often exhibited. These formations range from simple circles to intricate designs that incorporate advanced mathematical concepts. In this chapter, we delve into the mathematical and geometric intricacies of crop circles, exploring specific patterns, their evolution, and the theories attempting to decode their meanings.

## THE MATHEMATICS BEHIND CROP CIRCLES

### Geometric Precision

Many crop circles exhibit geometric precision that challenges our understanding of natural and human-made capabilities. Early formations were simple, often consisting of basic circles or rings. However, as the phenomenon evolved, the designs became increasingly sophisticated, demonstrating a deep understanding of geometric principles.

One notable example is the "Flower of Life", part of a series of patterns known as sacred geometry. This is a pattern consisting of multiple evenly spaced, overlapping circles arranged in a 6-fold flower-like design. This pattern, which appears in various cultural and historical contexts, signifies unity and the interconnectedness of life. The precision required to create such a pattern in a crop field, often overnight, suggests advanced planning and execution skills.

### Mathematical Complexity

Crop circles also exhibit a remarkable level of mathematical complexity. Patterns such as the "Julia Set" and "Mandelbrot Set" are prime examples. These designs are fractals, mathematical sets that display self-similarity at different scales. The Julia Set, for instance, is a complex fractal pattern that requires an understanding of advanced mathematical concepts to create. The Mandelbrot Set, another well-known fractal, is characterized by its infinitely complex boundary. Creating a representation of this set in a crop field with such precision is a feat that suggests a sophisticated understanding of mathematics.

# THE GEOMETRIC PATTERNS OF CROP CIRCLES

### Simple Shapes
Simple shapes are the foundation of more complex crop circle designs. Common shapes such as circles, lines, and spirals are frequently observed in crop circles. These basic forms often serve as the building blocks for more intricate patterns.

For example, the circle is a universal symbol representing unity, wholeness, and infinity. Its frequent appearance in crop circles might signify these concepts, suggesting a message of universal importance. Spirals, on the other hand, symbolize growth and evolution, hinting at the dynamic nature of life and the universe.

### Complex Designs
As the phenomenon of crop circles evolved, the designs became more complex, incorporating intricate geometric shapes and patterns. The "Milk Hill Galaxy Spiral" (2001) for instance, is a massive spiral formation consisting of hundreds of individual circles arranged with precise spacing and alignment. This formation, which appeared overnight, demonstrates a level of complexity that challenges conventional explanations.

Similarly, the "Barbury Castle Trinary Formation" (1991) is an intricate design featuring multiple geometric elements, including triangles, circles, and lines. The precision and scale of these designs suggest advanced techniques and tools, raising questions about their origin.

# SIGNIFICANT CROP CIRCLE PATTERNS

### The Hydrogen Symbol
One recurring symbol in crop circles is the hydrogen atom, representing the most basic and abundant element in the universe. The hydrogen symbol typically appears as a simple circle with a single proton and electron. Its frequent appearance in crop circles suggests it may carry a significant message, possibly related to the fundamental building blocks of life.

### The Carbon-Based Life Symbol
Another significant symbol is the carbon-based life symbol, often depicted as a methane molecule ($CH_4$). This symbol represents carbon-based life forms, which include all known biological organisms on Earth. The recurring appearance of this symbol in crop circles highlights the importance of carbon as a foundation for life, hinting at a deeper connection to the origins of life.

### Notched Spiral Numeracy
The notched spiral is another recurring theme in crop circles, often representing mathematical concepts. The "Barbury Castle Trinary" formation (1991) and the "Geometric PI Representation" (2008) are notable examples. The "Barbury Castle Trinary" formation features a complex arrangement of circles and lines that encode mathematical information, such as the golden ratio or Fibonacci sequence. These patterns suggest a sophisticated understanding of numeracy and geometry.

## THE EVOLUTION OF PATTERNS

### Early Simple Patterns
Historical records show that early crop circles were relatively simple in design. Early examples from the late 20th century often featured basic circles or rings, which captured public attention and curiosity. These simple patterns laid the foundation for the more intricate designs that would follow.

### Recent Complex Patterns
In recent years, crop circles have continued to evolve, displaying even greater complexity and sophistication. Patterns such as the "Kozvarce Sacred Geometry" (2012) and "Star Map Formation" (2014) showcase advanced geometric and mathematical principles, often appearing overnight with stunning precision. These recent developments suggest an ongoing evolution in the creation and purpose of crop circles, potentially representing an attempt to convey more intricate messages or information.

**ROUNDWAY HILL, WILTSHIRE, UK**

## JULY 2014

# THE INTERPRETATION OF PATTERNS

## Symbolic Meanings
The symbolic meanings of crop circle patterns are a topic of much speculation and debate. Some researchers believe that crop circles contain symbolic messages related to spirituality, science, or universal truths. For instance, the repeated appearance of the hydrogen and carbon symbols might signify messages about the fundamental nature of life and the universe.

Insights from experts in fields such as mathematics, physics, and art provide valuable perspectives on the potential meanings and significance of these patterns. Their interpretations can help decode the symbolic language of crop circles, offering a deeper understanding of their purpose.

## Communication Theories
One of the most intriguing theories is that crop circles are a form of communication from a higher intelligence. Proponents of this theory suggest that crop circles may be a way for extraterrestrial or non-human intelligences to communicate with humanity. The use of complex geometric and mathematical patterns could be an attempt to convey information in a universal language that transcends cultural and linguistic barriers.

If crop circles are indeed a form of communication, this raises profound questions about the nature of the messages being conveyed and the intentions of the entities creating them. Are they attempting to share knowledge, warn us of impending dangers, or simply make contact?

**SACRED GEOMETRY, NOTCHED SPIRAL & HYDROGEN SIGNATURE**
**KOZAROVCE, SLOVAKIA**
**JULY 2009**

# CHALLENGES IN UNDERSTANDING PATTERNS

## Complexity and Scale
Understanding and interpreting the complex patterns found in crop circles presents significant challenges. The intricate designs and mathematical precision of many crop circles require a high level of expertise to decode and understand fully. The large scale of some crop circles, combined with their sudden appearance, makes them difficult to study and analyze in detail.

## Mathematics & Geometry
The mathematical and geometric patterns of crop circles represent one of the most intriguing aspects of this phenomenon. The precision, layered meaning and complexity of these designs suggest a deeper significance and raise questions about their origin and purpose.

## Human vs. Non-Human Origins
The debate over whether crop circles are human-made or of non-human origin continues to be a central issue. Human-made theories suggest that crop circles are created by skilled artists or pranksters using advanced techniques. Non-human theories propose that they are created by extraterrestrial or other higher intelligences. Both sides present compelling evidence, but the sheer complexity and precision of some crop circles challenge conventional explanations and suggest the possibility of non-human origins.

# CHAPTER 9: POTENTIAL DECRYPTION KEYS & LANGUAGE STRUCTURE

The exploration of crop circles has revealed several recurring symbols and patterns that may serve as decryption keys to unlock their meaning. Among these, the hydrogen signature stands out as a critical element, suggesting a sophisticated understanding of both scientific principles and symbolic communication. This chapter delves into the hydrogen signature and other significant patterns that offer potential keys to deciphering the messages encoded in crop circles.

## THE HYDROGEN SIGNATURE

Hydrogen, the most abundant element in the universe, plays a crucial role in many crop circle formations. Its recurring presence suggests a deliberate choice, possibly indicating its fundamental importance in the communication from higher intelligence. The hydrogen atom, with its simple yet profound structure, is a universal symbol that transcends linguistic and cultural barriers, making it ideal for conveying messages across varied intelligences.

**Recurrence and Patterns**
The hydrogen signature appears frequently in crop circles, often as a central element around which other patterns are structured. For instance, the Barbury Castle trinary formation, one of the most famous crop circles, prominently features a representation of the hydrogen atom. This recurrence indicates that hydrogen may be a foundational element in the symbolic language of crop circles and is key to understanding more complex messages.

**Symbolism and Interpretation**
Hydrogen's simplicity and universality make it a powerful symbol. It represents the beginning of the periodic table and the building block of all matter. In the context of crop circles, the hydrogen signature could signify the origins of life, the interconnectedness of the universe, or a common foundation shared by all intelligent beings. Its repeated appearance suggests that the message being conveyed is fundamental to understanding the nature of existence and our place within the cosmos.

# BARBURY CASTLE TRINARY FORMATION (1991)

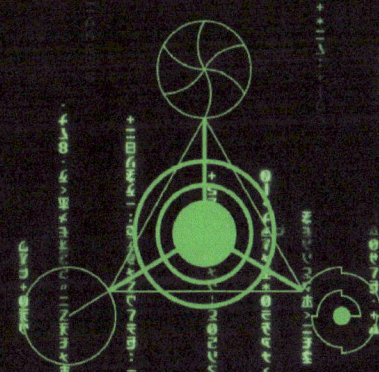

"The Barbury Castle trinary formation", discovered in 1991, is one of the most studied and celebrated crop circles. It features a complex design that incorporates three distinct sections, each representing different aspects of a trinary code. This formation is often cited as evidence of advanced mathematical and symbolic communication.

The trinary code within the Barbury Castle formation has been interpreted as a message related to fundamental physical constants, such as the speed of light, the Planck constant, and the gravitational constant. These interpretations suggest that the formation is not merely artistic but also encodes significant scientific information. The precise geometry and mathematical relationships within the formation point to a level of sophistication that challenges conventional explanations.

# THE NOTCHED SPIRAL NUMERACY CONCEPT

**Concept and Design**
The notched spiral numeracy concept is another recurring element in crop circles, characterized by spirals with evenly spaced notches or segments. These designs often incorporate mathematical constants, such as pi, and can be interpreted as visual representations of numerical sequences or algorithms.

**Mathematical Significance**
The notched spiral patterns highlight the use of advanced mathematical principles in crop circle design. These formations suggest an understanding of complex mathematical concepts and their visual representation. The precise spacing and alignment of the notches indicate a deliberate encoding of numerical information, potentially serving as a key to decrypting more intricate messages within the formations.

# CORRELATION WITH HIGHER INTELLIGENCE

### Advanced Scientific Knowledge
The presence of the hydrogen signature, trinary codes, and notched spiral patterns indicates a level of scientific knowledge that surpasses typical human understanding. These elements suggest that the creators of crop circles possess an advanced understanding of both physical laws and mathematical principles, pointing to a higher intelligence behind the formations.

### Intentional Communication
The deliberate use of universal symbols, such as hydrogen, and complex mathematical patterns indicates an intention to communicate with humanity. The choice of these symbols suggests that the message is meant to be accessible to those with a certain level of scientific and mathematical knowledge, encouraging further investigation and discovery.

### Implications for Human Understanding
The study of these potential decryption keys opens new avenues for understanding the nature of intelligence and communication. It challenges us to expand our knowledge and consider the possibility of contact with higher intelligences. The recurring symbols and patterns in crop circles offer a glimpse into a sophisticated form of communication that transcends traditional language barriers, inviting us to explore the deeper meanings encoded within these formations.

## SACRED GEOMETRY, NOTCHED SPIRAL & HYDROGEN SIGNATURE
### KOZAROVCE, SLOVAKIA
# JULY 2009

**THIS NOTCHED SPIRAL INDICATES NUMERIC REPRESENTATION**

# CHAPTER 10: NOVEL MATHEMATICAL EQUATION REPRESENTATIONS

Some interesting novel mathematical equation representations have appeared in crop circle formations, suggesting a highly sophisticated level of intelligence behind their creation and is something we might expect to see in messages from a higher intelligence. These patterns, which often incorporate fundamental mathematical concepts and geometric principles, point to the possibility of a higher intelligence attempting to communicate through a universal language. This chapter delves into notable examples of these novel mathematical representations found in crop circles, emphasizing their potential as signals from a higher intelligence.

## GEOMETRIC REPRESENTATION OF PI (2008)

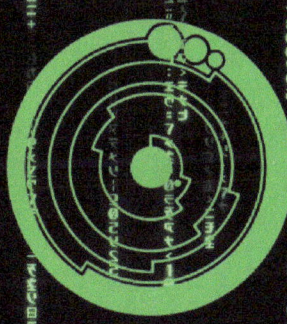

The representation of the mathematical constant π (Pi) in crop circles is an example of the use of sacred geometry to convey complex information.

### Concept and Appearance

The geometric representation of PI as depicted here appeared at a common crop circle location: Barbury Castle in 2008. This formation depicted a spiral with segments representing the digits of PI. The design included a series of curved lines and dots that accurately encoded the first ten digits of Pi, demonstrating a precise understanding of this fundamental mathematical constant.

### Interpretation

- Mathematical Precision: The accurate representation of Pi in a crop circle suggests a level of mathematical knowledge that surpasses casual or random creation. The use of Pi, a universal mathematical constant, indicates

an advanced intelligence familiar with fundamental principles of mathematics.
- Universal Language: Mathematics is often considered a universal language, transcending cultural and linguistic barriers. The use of the numeric notched spiral as seen in other formations, is more clear evidence of a language.

# EULER'S IDENTITY BINARY DISC (2010)

Euler's identity, a remarkable equation in mathematics, has also appeared in a novel crop circle formation, further supporting the idea of highly intelligent design.

**Concept and Appearance**
This notable crop circle formation appeared in 2010, a novel <u>binary disc pattern that encoded Euler's identity</u>: $e^{(i\pi)} + 1 = 0$. This formation used a series of dots and lines to represent the components of the equation in binary code.

The formation's intricate design required a deep understanding of both the mathematical equation and binary encoding, showcasing a blend of advanced mathematical and computational knowledge.

**Interpretation**
Mathematical Significance: Euler's identity is renowned for its elegance and the way it links five fundamental mathematical constants. The appearance of this equation in a crop circle indicates a sophisticated level of mathematical comprehension.

**Binary Encoding**
The use of binary code to represent Euler's identity adds another layer of complexity and suggests an advanced method of communication. Binary code is foundational in computing and digital communication, pointing to a technologically advanced intelligence.

# FRACTAL PATTERN SERIES

Fractal patterns, which are complex structures that exhibit self-similarity across different scales, have been frequently observed in crop circles.

## Concept and Appearance
Crop circles featuring fractal patterns, such as the Mandelbrot Set and Julia Set, have captivated researchers. These patterns are known for their intricate, repeating designs that reflect mathematical principles of self-similarity and scaling.

Notable formations include the 1996 "Julia Set" near Stonehenge, which displayed a series of circles arranged in a fractal pattern, and the 1991 "Mandelbrot Set" formation, which mirrored the famous fractal shape discovered by mathematician Benoît Mandelbrot.

## Mathematical Complexity
Fractals are complex mathematical structures that require sophisticated understanding to create. The presence of fractal patterns in crop circles suggests an advanced knowledge of mathematics and geometry.

## Symbolic Communication
Fractals symbolize order within chaos and are found throughout nature, from snowflakes to coastlines. Their use in crop circles may signify an attempt to communicate using natural and mathematical symbols that convey deeper meanings.

## Evidence of Higher Intelligence
The ability to create accurate and complex fractal patterns in crop circles implies a level of intelligence and technological capability that surpasses human pranksters or natural explanations. This strongly supports the theory of higher intelligence involved in the creation of these formations.

# CYMATIC PATTERN SERIES

Cymatics, the study of visible sound vibrations, has also been represented in crop circles, suggesting a connection between sound frequencies and geometric patterns.

### Concept and Appearance
Cymatic patterns in crop circles often resemble the geometric shapes created by sound waves vibrating through a medium, such as sand on a Chladni plate. These patterns, known as "Chladni figures," have appeared in several crop circle formations.

Notable examples include the 2001 series of formations; several complex cymatic patterns appeared resembling those produced by specific sound frequencies. It would be interesting to note the size of the formations or if there is any uniformity in size this could be indicative of a precise ratio that may be used to reproduce the patterns.

### Sound and Geometry
Cymatic patterns demonstrate the relationship between sound frequencies and geometric shapes. Their presence in crop circles suggests an understanding of how sound waves can create structured patterns, indicating an advanced knowledge of acoustics and geometry.

### Universal Connection
Cymatics may bridge the gap between sound and visual geometry, offering potential for a universal means of communication. The use of cymatic patterns in crop circles may represent an attempt to convey information through universally recognizable patterns.

# CHAPTER 11: DETECTING & DECODING MESSAGES FROM POTENTIAL HIGHER INTELLIGENCES

Understanding what messages from a higher intelligence might look like is crucial in interpreting crop circles. This chapter explores the key elements we might expect to see in such messages, and examines how various crop circle patterns, including the Hydrogen Signature and the Arecibo Response, align with these expectations. By comparing these patterns to known scientific symbols and efforts like the Pioneer Plaque, we can gain insights into the potential communication strategies of advanced civilizations.

## WHAT WE CAN EXPECT TO SEE IN MESSAGES FROM A HIGHER INTELLIGENCE

### Universal Symbols
- Mathematical and Geometric Precision: Messages might use universal mathematical and geometric patterns, understood by any intelligent civilization. This includes prime numbers, fractals, and geometric shapes.
- Elemental Symbols: Symbols representing fundamental elements, such as hydrogen, which is the most abundant element in the universe.

### Scientific Information
- Basic Biological Data: Information about the sending species' biology, similar to the human DNA data sent in the Arecibo message.
- Astronomical Information: Data about their star system or planet, potentially mirroring our own solar system or astronomical coordinates.

### Technological Signatures
- Technological Blueprints: Representations of their technological advancements or communication devices.
- Frequency References: Specific frequencies or signals used for communication, akin to the hydrogen line frequency.

## WHY CHOOSE THE MEDIUM OF CROPS?

The use of crops as a medium for communication is both novel and ingenious. Unlike radio waves, which could interfere with our own communications and potentially reveal the origin of the signal, crop circles offer a non-intrusive, pictorial method of conveying messages. This method requires a level of technical advancement and an understanding of both our technological capabilities and the environment. It suggests a higher intelligence that is aware of our limitations and chooses to communicate in a way that minimizes disruption. Using crops to create intricate patterns can be seen as akin to how we might attempt to communicate with species that we may regard as being of lower intelligence, such as chimpanzees or dogs. Just as we use visual symbols and basic tools to engage with animals, these crop circles could be the equivalent from a more advanced intelligence reaching out to humanity. This approach respects our current technological level while encouraging us to decipher and understand the messages conveyed through these remarkable formations.

## THE HYDROGEN SIGNATURE

The Hydrogen Signature in crop circles is a recurring pattern that aligns with the expectations of messages from higher intelligence. Hydrogen, being the most common element in the universe, is a logical choice for establishing a universal means of communication.

### Historical Context and Appearances
The Hydrogen Signature has been a prominent feature in crop circles since the late 20th century. One of the earliest significant appearances was in Wiltshire, England, in the early 1990s. Its consistent recurrence suggests deliberate use as a universal symbol.

### SETI and the Hydrogen Line
The search for extraterrestrial intelligence (SETI) focuses on the hydrogen line frequency at 1420 MHz. This frequency is thought to be a likely candidate for interstellar communication due to the abundance of hydrogen in the universe. The recurring Hydrogen Signature in crop circles reinforces the idea of using hydrogen as a common ground for communication.

# THE ARECIBO RESPONSE

Background In 1974, the Arecibo Observatory transmitted a message designed by Dr. Frank Drake and Carl Sagan, aimed at the M13 star cluster. The message included information about humanity and Earth, encoded in binary form.

- The Crop Circle Response In 2001, a crop circle appeared near the Chilbolton radio telescope in Hampshire, England, that seemed to be a response to the Arecibo message. This formation included:
- A Human-like Figure: Depicting the senders' appearance.
- Solar System Diagram: Very similar to ours, indicating their planetary system is either very similar or they inhabit our solar system, specifically Earth, Mars and Saturn.
- DNA Sequences: Suggesting biological differences.
Communication Device: A pattern resembling the Arecibo message's depiction of our radio telescope.

### Analysis and Implications
The Chilbolton crop circle's details suggest an understanding of our message and a deliberate attempt to respond. This supports the idea of crop circles being used for interstellar communication.

# THE PIONEER PLAQUE & UNIVERSAL SYMBOLS

The Pioneer Plaque Attached to the Pioneer 10 and 11 spacecraft, the plaque designed by Carl Sagan and Frank Drake included:

- The Hydrogen Atom Transition: Serving as a universal constant.
- Human Figures: Indicating the appearance of humans.
- Solar System Diagram: Showing the planets and the spacecraft's origin.

### Comparison to Crop Circles
Crop circles often feature similar universal symbols:
- Hydrogen Signatures: Mirroring the plaque's hydrogen atom depiction.
- Geometric Patterns: Suggesting mathematical knowledge.
- Astronomical Symbols: Representing solar systems or star constellations.

## OTHER NOTABLE PATTERNS

Cymatic Series (2001): The Cymatic Series of 2001 depicted intricate cymatic patterns, which are visual representations of sound vibrations. One notable formation was an octahedral pattern composed of eight five-pointed stars. This aligns with the idea of using universal patterns to convey complex information.

Roswell Rock Formation (1996): In 1996, a crop circle appeared depicting cycles of an eclipse sequence. Eight years later, a rock inscribed with the same pattern was found near Roswell, New Mexico, the site of the famous 1947 UFO incident. The origins of the rock and its means of construction are unknown, but its appearance years before in a crop field suggests a connection rather than a coincidence.

Signal Transmitter Depiction (2000): A crop circle appearing in 2000 depicted a detailed image of what looked like a signal transmitter. This pattern reappeared as part of the Arecibo Response in 2001, suggesting the use of technology similar to ours for communication.

The Carbon Signature: Similar to the Hydrogen Signature, the Carbon Signature appears in various crop circles, representing carbon, a fundamental element in all known life forms. Its recurring presence suggests an attempt to highlight the building blocks of life, potentially offering clues about the senders' biology.

Fractal Series: Fractals are complex patterns that are self-similar across different scales. The appearance of fractal designs in crop circles, such as the famous Mandelbrot Set, indicates a sophisticated understanding of mathematical concepts and suggests the use of universal patterns to convey messages.

**Overall Language Hints**
Many crop circles incorporate symbols and patterns that hint at a larger, coherent language. These designs often feature repeated motifs and consistent themes, suggesting an underlying structure akin to a language or code that we have yet to fully decipher.

# CHAPTER 12: LIGHT ORB PHENOMENA

One of the most captivating aspects of the crop circle phenomena is the frequent association with mysterious light orbs. These orbs, often reported as glowing spheres or "balls of light" (BOLs), have been witnessed in and around crop circle formations for decades. The light orb phenomena adds another layer of intrigue to the already mysterious crop circles, suggesting a potential connection between these lights and the creation of the formations. This chapter delves into a crucial piece of evidence: a 1991 witness report made to UK police, later disclosed under the Freedom of Information Act (FOIA) in 2008, which detailed the creation of a crop circle by a "whirlwind of light orbs". This report not only provides compelling evidence for an otherworldly origin for crop circles, but the timing also raises major questions about a possible government cover-up involving the infamous Doug and Dave.

## DISCLOSURE OF THE 1991 EYE-WITNESS REPORT

### The Incident
In June 1991, a couple in Wiltshire, UK, pulled over on the side of the road to report an extraordinary sight to the local police. According to the witnesses, a formation appeared in the field following a night of other unusual activity in the area. The couple described seeing a "whirlwind of light orbs", 4 in total, moving rapidly and seemingly intelligently through the field. These light orbs, they claimed, were responsible for creating an intricate crop circle pattern that was discovered in the same field the following morning.

### Official Documentation
The incident was officially documented by the UK police, and the report was later disclosed under the FOIA in 2008. The details of the report are striking:

- Date and Time: The incident occurred on the night of June 14, 1991.
- Location: A wheat field near Alton Barnes, Wiltshire.
- Description: The witnesses described multiple light orbs moving in a coordinated fashion, creating complex geometric patterns in the crops.
- Police Response: Local authorities took the report seriously, visiting the site and documenting the formation.

## Government Knowledge

The disclosure of this report under the FOIA suggests that the UK government was aware of potential role of the light orb phenomena in crop circle creation. Despite this, there was no public acknowledgment or investigation into these claims at the time, further hinting at a potential cover up.

# THE FOLLOWING MEDIA PSY-OP?

### Timing of The Doug and Dave Revelation

In September 1991, just three months after the Wiltshire incident, Doug Bower and Dave Chorley came forward, claiming responsibility for many of the crop circles in England. Their story was widely publicized, and they demonstrated their technique using simple tools like planks and ropes. The media quickly embraced this explanation, which effectively quelled public speculation about more mysterious origins.

### Challenging the Official Narrative

The timing of Doug and Dave's revelation is suspiciously convenient. It followed closely after the Wiltshire report, raising questions about whether their story was part of a deliberate disinformation campaign. If the government knew about the light orb phenomenon, why promote the hoax explanation so fervently?

Media Coverage: The media's immediate acceptance of Doug and Dave's story suggests a coordinated effort to provide a simple explanation to the public.

Lack of Scrutiny: Despite their claims, Doug and Dave failed to replicate the complexity of many crop circles and changed their story multiple times, yet their explanation went largely unchallenged.

# PROMINENT HUMAN ARTISTS & LIGHT ORBS

Interestingly, even some prominent human circle makers and hardened skeptics have admitted to seeing light orbs in fields while creating formations. This suggests that the light orbs might be monitoring or even interacting with the human creators, indicating that higher intelligence (or technology) could be listening for responses or observing human behavior in the fields.

# THE DISCLOSED REPORT & ITS IMPLICATIONS

**Evidence of Light Orb Involvement**
The Wiltshire report provides compelling evidence that light orbs may play a role in crop circle creation. The detailed eyewitness account, supported by official documentation, highlights several key points:

- Intelligent Behavior: The light orbs moved in a coordinated manner, suggesting intelligence or control.

- Complex Patterns: The resulting crop circle was intricate, far beyond the capabilities of simple tools like those used by Doug and Dave.

- Government Awareness: The fact that this report was documented and later released indicates that authorities were aware of and potentially investigating these phenomena.

**Cover-Up and Disinformation**
The potential cover-up and disinformation campaign involving Doug and Dave raises serious questions about the true origins of crop circles. If the government knew about the light orb phenomenon, promoting a simple hoax explanation could serve several purposes:

- Public Reassurance: Providing a mundane explanation would prevent public panic or fascination with potentially extraterrestrial or advanced technological phenomena.

- Distraction: The Doug and Dave story could distract from genuine investigations and discourage serious scientific inquiry into crop circles.

- Control of Narrative: By controlling the narrative, authorities could manage public perception and maintain secrecy around unexplained phenomena.

## CHRIS BLEDSOE'S ENCOUNTERS

One of the most compelling and well-documented cases of interaction with light orbs comes from Chris Bledsoe, a North Carolina resident who has experienced numerous encounters with these enigmatic entities. Bledsoe's interactions with light orbs began in 2007, and over the years, he has amassed a significant amount of evidence, including photographs, videos, and personal testimonies. His experiences have drawn the attention of various researchers and various government agencies, including the CIA.

Bledsoe's encounters often involve close-up observations of the orbs, which he describes as exhibiting intelligent behavior. They respond to his presence, sometimes following him or appearing to communicate through light signals. These interactions suggest that the orbs are not only real but also possess a level of intelligence that allows them to interact with humans in meaningful ways. The interest from government agencies further validates the significance of Bledsoe's experiences, indicating that there is more to the phenomenon than mere folklore or optical illusions.

## STEVEN GREER & THE CE5 PROTOCOL

Dr. Steven Greer, a prominent figure in the UFO and extraterrestrial research community, has developed a protocol known as CE5, which stands for Close Encounters of the Fifth Kind. This protocol involves human-initiated contact with extraterrestrial intelligence through a combination of meditation, visualization, and coherent thought sequencing. Greer claims that by using CE5,

groups of people using the power of the mind can manifest sightings of UFOs and light orbs, and can even result in the formation of crop circle patterns.

## Manifesting Light Orbs and Crop Circles

Greer has documented numerous instances where CE5 protocols reportedly led to sightings of light orbs and the formation of crop circles. These experiments often involve groups of participants who gather in specific locations, engage in meditation, and project thoughts and intentions aimed at making contact with extraterrestrial beings. According to Greer, these sessions have resulted in:

- Light Orb Sightings: Participants have reported seeing light orbs appearing in the sky and interacting with the group.

- Crop Circle Formations: In some cases, new crop circle formations have been discovered in fields near the meditation sites shortly after CE5 sessions.

## Implications of CE5

If Greer's claims are accurate, they suggest a direct method for humans to communicate and interact with the intelligences behind the light orbs and crop circles using the power of prayer and collective consciousness. This would provide a powerful tool for researchers seeking to understand these phenomena and could lead to breakthroughs in our understanding of extraterrestrial technology and intentions, consciousness and the nature of our reality.

## THE LIGHT ORB PHENOMENA SUMMARY

The 1991 witness report from Wiltshire, detailing the creation of a crop circle by a "whirlwind of light orbs", is a pivotal piece of evidence in understanding the true origin of crop circles. It suggests that the UK government may have been aware of the role of the light orb phenomenon in crop circle creation just a few short months prior to the public revelation by Doug and Dave. The timing and promotion of Doug and Dave's story raise serious questions about a potential government cover-up and disinformation campaign. As we continue to explore the mysteries of crop circles, it is crucial to re-examine such evidence and consider the broader implications for our understanding.

# CHAPTER 13: ROLE OF MEDIA & PUBLIC PERCEPTION

Media has played a pivotal role in shaping public perception of crop circles, often steering the narrative towards skepticism and dismissing legitimate research. This chapter delves into how media coverage has facilitated a cover-up of the crop circle phenomenon, the infamous Colin Andrews media debacle, and the broader implications of media manipulation on public understanding and scientific inquiry.

## EARLY MEDIA COVERAGE

### Initial Reports and Sensationalism
In the early days of crop circle appearances, media coverage was often sensationalist. Newspapers and television programs reported on the strange patterns with a mix of curiosity and skepticism, frequently framing the phenomenon as a curiosity or a hoax. The Westbury White Horse crop circle, for example, received widespread media attention in the late 1970s, sparking public interest and debate.

### The Role of Local Media
Local media outlets played a crucial role in documenting early crop circles. Farmers and locals would report new formations to local newspapers, which then disseminated the information to a broader audience. This grassroots level of reporting helped build a foundational understanding of crop circles and brought them to the attention of national and international media.

## THE COLIN ANDREWS MEDIA DEBACLE

### Attempted Documentation Sabotage
Colin Andrews, a prominent crop circle researcher, faced significant challenges in his efforts to document crop circle formations. During a highly publicized attempt to record a crop circle being formed, Andrews and his team were thwarted by "pranksters" who sabotaged their efforts. This incident was widely covered in the media, furthering the narrative that crop circles were merely the work of human hoaxers.

## Military Involvement and Separate Testing

While the public was led to believe that Andrews' efforts were futile, the military took the phenomenon of crop circles seriously. Behind the scenes, they conducted their own tests in private fields, away from the prying eyes of the media and the public. These covert operations indicate that certain authorities recognized the potential significance of crop circles and were intent on conducting their own investigations away from public scrutiny.

# THE DOUG & DAVE DEBACLE

## The Prankster Claim

In the late 1980s, Doug Bower and Dave Chorley claimed responsibility for many crop circles, demonstrating their technique with planks and ropes. Their story was widely publicized, and the media quickly adopted the narrative that most, if not all, crop circles were the result of human pranksters. This explanation was convenient and widely accepted, overshadowing more serious research efforts.

## Colin Andrews' Challenge

Colin Andrews, skeptical of Bower and Chorley's claims, challenged them to replicate even a simple crop circle pattern under controlled conditions. Despite their bravado, Bower and Chorley failed to produce a convincing result, casting doubt on their ability to create the more complex formations. This incident, however, received far less media attention than their initial claims, illustrating how media coverage often favored the debunking narrative.

# MEDIA MANIPULATION & PUBLIC PERCEPTION

## The Role of Sensationalism

Media coverage of crop circles has often leaned heavily on sensationalism, focusing on the most bizarre and unexplainable aspects of the phenomenon. This approach has both captivated the public and fueled skepticism, making it difficult for serious research to gain traction. Sensationalist stories attract viewership but often at the cost of nuanced understanding and scientific inquiry.

## Misinformation and Disinformation

The media's tendency to highlight hoaxes and debunking efforts has contributed to widespread misinformation about crop circles. Instances of deliberate disinformation campaigns, possibly orchestrated to discredit genuine research, have further muddied the waters. The Colin Andrews debacle and the propagation of the Doug and Dave edxplaination are prime examples of how media can be used to manipulate public perception and obscure the truth.

# CASE STUDIES

### The "Warminster Thing"

The "Warminster Thing" is a notable case study in media influence. During the 1960s and 1970s, a series of unexplained phenomena, including crop circles, were reported in Warminster, England. Media coverage transformed the town into a hub for UFO enthusiasts and researchers. However, the media frenzy also led to increased skepticism and ridicule, complicating serious investigation efforts.

### The Oliver's Castle Video

The "Oliver's Castle" video from 1996 purported to show orbs of light creating a crop circle. This footage captured significant media attention, sparking intense debate within the crop circle community. While some hailed it as definitive proof of non-human involvement, others questioned its authenticity.

### Authenticity and Hoax Allegations

In the years following its release, the video's authenticity came under scrutiny. Footage emerged of a person claiming to have created the video, revealing that he was a professional CGI editor. Although this does not constitute solid proof, it seems likely that the video could have been hoaxed using computer-generated imagery.

## Context and Cover-Up Theories

Despite the hoax allegations, it's important to consider the broader context. The video appeared four years after a report surfaced of a whirlwind of light orbs creating crop circles. This earlier report was not public knowledge at the time the Oliver's Castle video was released. This temporal gap suggests the possibility that the video was created as a deliberate cover-up to discredit any future similar footage. This notion aligns with a common theme surrounding the crop circle phenomenon: efforts to obscure or undermine legitimate sightings and reports.

## Impact on Public Perception

The media coverage of the Oliver's Castle video highlights the power of compelling visual evidence to capture public imagination and influence perceptions. Even as the video's authenticity remains contested, it has left a lasting impact on the crop circle discourse. The video serves as a potent example of how visual evidence can both illuminate and complicate the quest for truth in the study of crop circles.

In summary, while the Oliver's Castle video is likely a hoax created by a professional CGI artist, its emergence within the context of prior, undisclosed reports of light orbs creating crop circles, suggests this could be part of a coordinated cover-up effort. This dynamic underscores the complexities of disentangling the genuine phenomena from hoaxes and fabricated evidence.

# THE ROLE OF MEDIA SUMMARY

The role of media in shaping public perception of crop circles is complex and multifaceted. While media coverage has brought attention to the phenomena, it has also facilitated a cover-up by promoting sensationalism and debunking narratives over serious scientific inquiry. The Colin Andrews media debacle and the propagation of the Doug and Dave explanation are stark reminders of how media can be used to manipulate public perception. By critically examining the impact of media on the crop circle phenomenon, we can better understand the ongoing challenges in uncovering the truth behind these enigmatic formations.

# CHAPTER 14: SCIENTIFIC INQUEST & PHYSICAL ANOMALIES

Scientific investigations into crop circles have revealed a host of intriguing anomalies that defy simple explanations. While the phenomenon is often dismissed by mainstream science, a closer examination of the physical and biological effects observed in crop circles suggests that there may be more to these formations than mere hoaxes or natural occurrences. This chapter delves into the scientific studies conducted on crop circles, exploring the physical changes in the crops, soil alterations, and the presence of unusual energy signatures.

## PHYSICAL CHANGES IN CROPS

### Altered Plant Structure

One of the most compelling areas of scientific inquiry involves the changes observed in the structure of the plants within crop circles. Studies have documented several unusual modifications:

- Elongated Nodes: Nodes, the knuckle-like structures along the stem of the plant, often appear elongated in crop circles. This elongation is not seen in crops outside the formations.

- Blown Nodes: Some crop circles exhibit nodes that appear "blown out," as if subjected to a sudden and intense burst of heat. This effect has been compared to the results of microwave radiation.

### Increased Growth Rates

Research has also indicated that crops within the formations sometimes show increased growth rates compared to their undisturbed counterparts. This phenomenon suggests that whatever causes the formation of crop circles might also stimulate the growth of plants, possibly through some form of energy or radiation.

## SOIL & ENVIRONMENTAL CHANGES

**Soil Composition**
Soil samples taken from crop circles have shown anomalies that differentiate them from control samples taken outside the formations. These differences include:

- Higher Levels of Magnetite: Some studies have found increased levels of magnetite in the soil within crop circles, suggesting the presence of unusual magnetic activity.

- Altered Mineral Composition: Changes in the mineral composition of the soil, including unusual concentrations of certain elements, have been observed.

**Radiation and Electromagnetic Fields**
Investigations have revealed elevated levels of radiation and unusual electromagnetic fields in and around crop circles. These findings include:

- Gamma Radiation: Some crop circles have shown increased levels of gamma radiation, which could indicate exposure to high-energy particles.

- Electromagnetic Anomalies: Devices such as compasses and electromagnetic field detectors often malfunction or show unusual readings within crop circles. This suggests the presence of strong and atypical electromagnetic fields.

## BIOPHYSICAL EFFECTS ON SEEDS

**Germination Rates**
Studies on the seeds collected from crop circles have shown significant biophysical effects. One of the most notable findings is the alteration in germination rates:

- Enhanced Germination: Seeds from some crop circles exhibit higher germination rates and more robust growth than seeds from outside the formations.

- Delayed Germination: In contrast, some formations result in seeds that show delayed germination, indicating that different mechanisms might be at play in different crop circles.

## DNA Alterations
Preliminary research has suggested that the DNA of plants from crop circles might undergo changes. These changes include:

- Increased Mutation Rates: Some studies have reported higher mutation rates in the DNA of plants from crop circles, which could be a response to exposure to unusual energies or environmental conditions.

- Epigenetic Changes: There is also evidence of epigenetic changes, which affect how genes are expressed without altering the underlying DNA sequence. These changes might be a plant's response to the stress or energy associated with the formation of crop circles.

# ENERGETIC & GEOPHYSICAL ANOMALIES

## Energy Signatures
Crop circles often exhibit unique energy signatures that can be detected using various instruments. These signatures include:

- Microwave Radiation: Some researchers have detected microwave radiation within crop circles, which could explain the elongated and blown nodes observed in the plants.

- Static Electricity: Elevated levels of static electricity have been recorded, suggesting that the formations might be associated with electrical phenomena.

## Acoustic Properties
Certain crop circles have been found to possess unusual acoustic properties. Experiments have shown that sound waves behave differently within crop circles, with some formations amplifying sound in specific ways. This has led to speculation that the shapes of crop circles might interact with sound waves or even be created by acoustic forces.

### Persistent Ghost Patterns

Many crop circles exhibit a phenomina known as ghost circles, this is where the pattern persists through future plantations. It is thought that this may be a result of people visiting the pattern and treading seeds into the ground.

## LABORATORY REPLICATIONS & LIMITATIONS

Scientific attempts to replicate the effects observed in crop circles have met with mixed results. While some aspects, such as the elongated nodes, can be reproduced using microwave radiation, other phenomena remain elusive. These challenges highlight the complexity of the crop circle phenomenon and suggest that multiple factors might be involved in their creation.

### Limitations of Current Research

Despite the intriguing findings, research into crop circles faces several limitations:

- Funding and Resources: Scientific investigation of crop circles is often underfunded and lacks the resources needed for comprehensive study.

- Skepticism and Bias: Mainstream scientific skepticism and bias against the phenomenon can hinder serious investigation and the publication of results.

- Variable Conditions: The variability of crop circles, with each formation exhibiting different characteristics, makes it difficult to develop a unified theory or explanation.

## SUMMARY OF THE SCIENTIFIC INQUEST

Scientific investigations into crop circles have uncovered a range of physical, biological, and energetic anomalies that challenge conventional explanations. From altered plant structures and unusual soil compositions to unique energy signatures and biophysical effects on seeds, the evidence suggests that crop circles are more than mere hoaxes or natural phenomena. While much remains to be understood, the scientific study of crop circles offers valuable insights into this enigmatic phenomena and underscores the need for continued research and open-minded inquiry.

# CHAPTER 15: APPARENT PREDICTIONS & FORECASTING OF THE FUTURE?

Skeptics of higher intelligence origins argue that the absence of clear, undeniable predictions of scientific discoveries or future occurrences undermines the hypothesis that crop circles are communications from an advanced civilization. They claim that if crop circles were indeed messages from a higher intelligence, we would expect them to contain information beyond our current understanding, offering glimpses into future technologies or significant events.

Despite these criticisms, there are notable instances that challenge this skeptical view. Within the vast array of crop circle formations, we find at least two compelling examples that appear to predict scientific advancements or events in ways that would be extraordinarily difficult, if not impossible, for humans to fabricate. These formations, analyzed thoroughly in this chapter, suggest that crop circles may indeed hold predictive power, aligning more closely with the hypothesis of higher intelligence origins.

This chapter delves into these intriguing cases, examining the evidence and implications of these predictions. By exploring these examples, we aim to provide a more nuanced understanding of the crop circle phenomenon, considering the possibility that some formations may indeed offer foresight into future developments, thereby supporting the theory of their extraterrestrial or higher intelligence origin.

## PREDICTIONS & APPARENT FOREKNOWLEDGE

Crop circles have occasionally displayed designs that suggest advanced knowledge of future scientific and technological milestones. This section explores several notable examples where crop circles appeared to predict or align with subsequent discoveries or events.

### Graphene Discovery (2003)

In 2003, a crop circle near Beckhampton and Milk Hill depicted a pattern resembling the structure of graphene, a single layer of carbon atoms

**2023** CROP PATTERN APPEARS TO PREDICT HURRICANE DORA CATEGORY AND DATE.

HURRICANE FORMED ON **31**ST JULY

PATTERN APPEARED ON **1**ST AUGUST

BRUSHES HAWAII ON **8**TH AUGUST

APPEARED ON PROHIBITED LAND OWNED BY MINISTRY OF DEFENCE

**2003** CROP PATTERN APPEARS TO PREDICT THE LATER DISCOVERY OF GRAPHENE IN **2004**

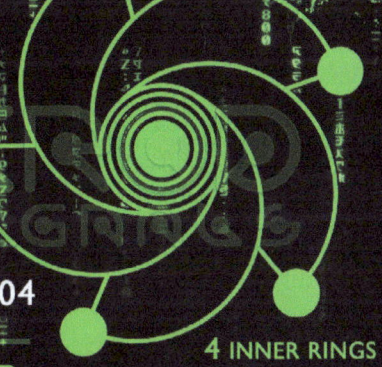

**4 INNER RINGS
CATEGORY 4 HURRICANE**

HOW DID THEY **KNOW?**

DEPICTS TESSALATING GRAPHENE LATTICE

01/08 2023

10/08 2003

# THE APPARENT PREDICTIONS

EVERY MESSAGE WE HAVE EVER SENT OUT IN SEARCH OF NON-HUMAN INTELLIGENCE HAS BEEN RESPONDED TO IN CROP FIELD PATTERNS.

WE THINK THERE ARE MANY MORE PATTERNS THAT HAVE NOT YET BEEN DECODED.

FIND OUT MORE ON...

**CROP SIGNALS**

CROPSIGNALS.APP

arranged in a two-dimensional honeycomb lattice. This formation appeared the year preceding the discovery of graphene in 2004, meaning either this is an extremely unlikely coincidence or a level of understanding that defies any hoax explainations.

### Oumuamua Interstellar Spinning Object (2017)

The appearance of a crop circle depicting a spinning, cigar-shaped object, resembling the characteristics of Oumuamua, an interstellar object detected in 2017, indicated an extraordinary level of prescient knowledge. The design mimicked the reported shape and motion of this mysterious object from beyond our solar system.

### Hurricane Season Start (2023)

On August 1st 2023 there was a crop circle formation appearing to depict a hurricane, interstingly this was the day after hurricane Dora, the first hurricane of the year, was detected, marking the beginning of hurricane season. What's curious also is that this formation appeared in a restricted field owned and monitored by the Ministry of Defence, further decreasing the likelihood of this being an elaborate hoax formation.

## ANALYSIS OF PREDICTIONS

To understand the implications of these predictions, we must assess the following aspects:
- Timing and Accuracy: Evaluating the precision of the crop circle designs in relation to the actual events or discoveries they purportedly predicted is crucial. Analyzing the timing and level of detail in the designs helps establish a correlation between the crop circles and subsequent real-world occurrences.
- Patterns and Trends: Identifying recurring patterns or trends in crop circle predictions provides insight into whether these formations follow a consistent methodology or if they reflect random coincidences. Analyzing the context and thematic elements of the predictions helps determine their relevance.
- Scientific and Technological Knowledge: Investigating the extent of scientific and technological knowledge reflected in the crop circles helps gauge their plausibility. This includes assessing the level of detail and accuracy in depicting complex concepts and phenomena.

## Potential Explanations for Predictive Aspects
Several hypotheses could explain the predictive nature of crop circles: Advanced Knowledge by Creators: If the crop circles are indeed the work of an advanced intelligence, it is possible that the creators possess knowledge far beyond current human understanding. This could include insights into future scientific and technological advancements.

## Pattern Recognition and Chance
Some researchers argue that the apparent predictions could be a result of pattern recognition and chance. Given the vast number of crop circles and the breadth of human scientific and technological inquiry, some coincidences may occur naturally.

## Influence of Information Leakages
Another possibility is that certain crop circles could have been influenced by leaked or insider information. In this scenario, individuals with access to advanced knowledge may have inadvertently contributed to the creation of predictive designs.

## Implications of Predictive Crop Circles
The apparent predictive nature of crop circles raises some major questions. If crop circles indeed predict uture events or discoveries, it suggests a level of intelligence and foresight that could be linked to extraterrestrial or higher-dimensional beings. This challenges our understanding of intelligence and communication beyond Earth.

## Impact on Scientific Inquiry
The presence of predictive crop circles could prompt a reevaluation of how scientific and technological advancements are perceived. If these formations accurately foresee future developments, they could inspire new approaches to research and exploration.

## Societal and Cultural Reactions
Predictive crop circles could influence societal and cultural reactions to the phenomenon. They might prompt increased interest in the origins of these designs and lead to further investigations into their significance.

# CHAPTER 16: THE TEST PROPOSAL - USING THE SCIENTIFIC METHOD TO INVESTIGATE CROP CIRCLE ORIGINS

Numerous reports and eyewitness accounts describe mysterious light orbs in the vicinity of crop circle formations, this includes some of the human artists while out in the fields. These accounts suggest not only a possible connection between these orbs and the creation of crop circles, but that the senders may be listening for responses.

This chapter proposes a scientific investigation, referred to as "The Test", designed to explore the hypothesis that crop circles are created by light orbs using advanced technology. By employing the scientific method, we aim to provide a structured and objective approach to understanding this phenomena.

## FORMULATING THE HYPOTHESIS

**Hypothesis**
Crop circles are created by light orbs using some form of advanced technology.

**Rationale**
This hypothesis is based on several key pieces of evidence:

- Eyewitness Reports: Numerous accounts from farmers, researchers, and locals describe seeing light orbs in fields where crop circles subsequently appeared.

- Police Reports: Law enforcement officers have also documented sightings of unexplained lights near crop circle sites and an report of a police officers encounter with what could very well have been 2 humanoid alien beings.

- Circle Makers' Testimonies: Some individuals who create crop circles for artistic purposes have reported encountering mysterious light orbs.

Given this context, it stands to reason that these light orbs may be involved in the creation of crop circles and may even be responding to or conveying messages.

## THE SCIENTIFIC METHOD APPLIED

### Observation
Before conducting "The Test", we should review and compile existing observations of light orbs and crop circle formations. This includes:
- Gathering eyewitness testimonies and police reports.
- Analyzing video footage and photographs of light orbs in crop circle fields.
- Studying the detailed accounts from circle makers who have reported interactions with these orbs.

### Research Question
Can we capture evidence of light orbs creating a crop circle by pre-encoding a message and using various communication techniques?

### Hypothesis
If light orbs are responsible for creating crop circles, then setting up a controlled environment with a pre-encoded message and monitoring it with high-definition cameras should result in capturing the creation process on video.

## EXPERIMENTAL DESIGN

### Variables
- Independent Variable: The presence of an encoded crop circle with a date and location.

- Dependent Variable: The appearance and activity of light orbs, and the creation of a new crop circle.

- Controlled Variables: Location, type of crop, weather conditions, time of year, and camera equipment.

## Procedure
- Permission and Preparation: Obtain permission from a farmer to create an encoded crop circle in their field. This will include a specific date and location.

- Encoding the Message: Design and create a crop circle with the encoded message using standard circle-making techniques to ensure it is indistinguishable from naturally occurring circles

- Camera Setup: Install high-definition cameras with night vision capabilities around the crop circle site. Ensure continuous recording for the duration specified in the encoded message.

- Communication Techniques: Combine the experiment with groups following CE5 protocols developed by Steven Greer, which are hypothesised to facilitate contact with extraterrestrial intelligence. Other communication methods may include broadcasting the encoded message using radio waves or light signals.

- Monitoring and Documentation: Continuously monitor the cameras and document any unusual activity, particularly the appearance of light orbs. Ensure that all equipment is regularly checked and maintained to prevent technical failures.

## DATA COLLECTION

Video Footage: Review the recorded footage for any signs of light orbs and the creation process of a new crop circle.

- Environmental Data: Record environmental conditions (e.g., weather, temperature) throughout the experiment.

- Witness Accounts: Collect testimonies from any individuals present during the experiment, including any CE5 group participants.

## Analysis
- Video Analysis: Analyze the footage for evidence of light orbs and the creation of crop circles. Look for patterns or anomalies that correlate with the encoded message.

- Correlation with Environmental Data: Examine whether certain environmental conditions coincide with the appearance of light orbs.
- Comparison with Historical Data: Compare findings with previous reports of light orb sightings and crop circle formations.

## Conclusion
Support or Refute Hypothesis: Determine whether the collected evidence supports the hypothesis that light orbs create crop circles.
Further Research: Suggest additional experiments or modifications to improve the study. Consider exploring different communication methods or locations.

## Publication and Peer Review
- Report Findings: Publish the results in a scientific journal or present them at conferences to invite scrutiny and feedback from the scientific community.
- Peer Review: Engage with other researchers to review and validate the findings, ensuring the study meets rigorous scientific standards.

## Hypothesis Variations
- Hypothesis 1: Light orbs create crop circles in response to encoded messages left in fields.
- Hypothesis 2: The presence of prayer groups following CE5 protocols increases the likelihood of light orbs creating crop circles.
- Hypothesis 3: Light orbs use advanced technology that can be detected with specific types of monitoring equipment (e.g., infrared cameras, electromagnetic field detectors).

# THE TEST PROPOSAL SUMMARY

By applying the scientific method to investigate the hypothesis that crop circles are created by light orbs using advanced technology, we aim to move beyond speculation and provide concrete evidence. "The Test" represents a structured approach to understanding a phenomenon that has puzzled researchers for decades. Whether the results confirm or refute the hypothesis, they will contribute valuable insights into the ongoing mystery of crop circles.

# CHAPTER 17: CONCLUSION & INTRO TO THE CROP SIGNALS PROJECT

The exploration of crop circles, from their historical origins to modern-day encounters, reveals a phenomenon rich with mystery and potential meaning. Throughout this book, we have examined various aspects of crop circles, including their possible natural explanations, human-made hoaxes, and the compelling evidence suggesting extraterrestrial or higher intelligence origins. As we conclude, it's essential to summarize the key insights and look forward to future investigations.

## SUMMARY OF KEY INSIGHTS

### Historical Context
Crop circles have a long and storied history, with references dating back to medieval times. These historical accounts, coupled with modern encounters, highlight the persistent and enigmatic nature of the phenomena.

### Complex Patterns and Symbols
The increasing complexity of crop circle designs, including geometric shapes, fractals, and mathematical representations, suggests a sophisticated understanding of both artistic and scientific principles. Symbols such as the hydrogen signature indicate a potential universal language aimed at communicating with us.

### Extraterrestrial and Higher Intelligence Theories
The correlation between crop circles and UFO sightings, coupled with specific cases like the Arecibo message response and the Roswell connections, points to the possibility of non-human origins. These theories propose that crop circles may be a form of communication from advanced intelligences.

## Challenges to Natural and Human-Made Explanations

While natural phenomena and human hoaxes account for some crop circles, the sheer complexity, precision, and occurrence in inaccessible locations challenge these explanations. The hoax theory, popularized by Doug and Dave, fails to account for many documented cases, especially those witnessed forming under extraordinary circumstances.

## Media and Government Involvement

The media's portrayal and certain government actions suggest a concerted effort to obscure or downplay the phenomenon. Incidents like the Colin Andrews debacle and the UK government's release of witness reports indicate a complex interplay of public perception and official response.

# THE DUALITY OF THE PHENOMENA

This book raises major questions about the crop circle phenomenon and strongly suggests that two separate phenomena are occurring: man-made art (either as a passion or cover-up operation) and signals from a higher intelligence. The methods that a higher intelligence might use to contact us could be so alien we fail to recognize them as such, maintaining plausible deniability for human authorities. The conclusions drawn point to two primary possibilities, neither of which can be fully ruled out:

## Entirely Man-Made

The phenomena could be the result of an incredibly sophisticated and prolonged art project carried out by teams of pranksters over the last 45 years. This would represent the most elaborate and sustained hoax in history. We also have to ignore all historical accounts and explain the logistical issues.

## Genuine Signals from a Higher Intelligence

Alternatively, we could be looking at authentic messages from a higher intelligence. The fact that some concepts in this book, such as the hydrogen signature, were first pointed out by the author of this book, rather than known hoaxers, and the improbability of such a vast and intricate hoax, lends considerable weight to this explanation.

Given the evidence and the analysis presented in this book, the latter explanation—that crop circles are signals from a higher intelligence—appears to be the more plausible conclusion. This journey to decode these enigmatic messages has only just begun, and future investigations will undoubtedly shed more light on this fascinating mystery. The potential implications for humanity are profound, suggesting that we may not be alone and that an advanced intelligence is reaching out to us in a subtle, yet unmistakable manner.

This book lays the groundwork for understanding the complex and multifaceted nature of crop circles and their potential "alien" origins. Future books in this series will build upon this foundation, delving deeper into specific areas of interest. Subsequent volumes will feature detailed analyses of individual crop circles, advanced decryption methods, and the latest findings from The Crop Signals Project. The ultimate goal is to demonstrate that crop circles could well be of higher intelligent origin and to develop a comprehensive understanding of these "Agrograms" and any potential implications for humanity, thereby fostering a new appreciation for this mysterious phenomenon and its potential as a medium for potential future communication protocols.

## UNIQUE INSIGHTS & NOVEL REVELATIONS

This book ventures beyond traditional narratives about crop circles, providing unique insights and groundbreaking revelations that challenge conventional thinking and invite readers to explore the mysterious phenomenon with a fresh perspective. Here are some of the novel revelations and insights offered within these pages:

### 1. Dual Nature of Crop Circles
We propose that the crop circle phenomenon encompasses two distinct types of formations: man-made art and genuine signals from higher intelligence. This dual nature suggests a complex interplay between human creativity and potential extraterrestrial communication, raising intriguing questions about the origins and purposes of these patterns.

## 2. Hydrogen Signature and Communication Evidence

The Hydrogen Signature crop circle aligns with principles used by the Search for Extraterrestrial Intelligence (SETI), underscoring its significance as a potential communication from advanced civilizations. This formation highlights how basic elements like hydrogen can serve as a universal language for interstellar messages.

## 3. Carbon Signature and Biological Indicators

The frequent appearance of the 4-fold circle formation, also known as the quintuplet, may symbolize carbon-based life (Methane, $CH_4$) or the fundamental building blocks of DNA. This pattern's recurrence and evolution suggest it could be a greeting from a silicon-based or other lifeforms, highlighting the versatility of DNA as a data storage medium.

## 4. Blueprint Series and Potential Technologies

The Blueprint Series of 2008 offers tantalizing glimpses of advanced technologies. These formations, resembling detailed technical schematics, may provide blueprints for anti-gravity devices or other cutting-edge technologies. The potential applications of these designs remain a fascinating area of exploration and experimentation.

## 5. Signal Device Depictions

The depiction of signal devices in crop circles, such as those found in the Arecibo Response, suggests a sophisticated understanding of communication technology. These formations appear to illustrate the mechanisms behind extraterrestrial broadcasts and the creation of crop circles themselves, offering insights into the technical capabilities of their creators.

## 6. Predictions and Scientific Advancements

While skeptics argue that crop circles lack predictions of future events or scientific advancements, this book presents at least two compelling examples where crop circle formations have foreshadowed scientific breakthroughs or events. The DNA disc formation, for instance, also predates the achievement of DNA as a method of data storage by several years.

## 7. Psychological and Energetic Phenomena

Visitors to crop circles often report experiencing strange electrical energies and altered states of consciousness. These psychological and energetic phenomena hint at a deeper, possibly intentional, interaction between the formations and human perception, inviting further study into the mind's role in interpreting and experiencing these patterns.

## 8. Government and Media Involvement

The book delves into the complex interplay between media portrayal, government actions, and public perception of crop circles. It examines incidents where media and governmental efforts may have been aimed at obscuring or discrediting genuine phenomena, highlighting the need for transparency and rigorous investigation.

## 9. Interdisciplinary Approach

By integrating insights from astrophysics, biology, psychology, and technology, this book offers a comprehensive and interdisciplinary approach to understanding crop circles. This holistic perspective encourages readers to consider multiple dimensions of the phenomenon, fostering a deeper appreciation for its complexity and potential significance.

## 10. Invitation for Further Exploration

Ultimately, this book serves as a call to action for researchers, enthusiasts, and the curious-minded to delve deeper into the study of crop circles. It sets the stage for future volumes that will explore advanced decryption methods, detailed analyses of individual formations, and the latest findings from ongoing research projects like The Crop Signals Project.

By presenting these unique insights and novel revelations, this book aims to transform our understanding of crop circles and inspire a new wave of exploration and discovery in this enigmatic field.

# INTRODUCTION TO THE CROP SIGNAL PROJECT

Given the compelling evidence and the need for a systematic approach to understanding crop circles, we have created <u>The Crop Signal Project</u>. This initiative aims to decode the meaning behind crop circles, assuming a higher intelligence origin, and to develop a comprehensive dictionary for scientific interpretation of the patterns.

## Objectives and Mission

The primary objectives of The Crop Signal Project are:
- Decoding Crop Circles: To analyze and interpret crop circle formations, focusing on recurring symbols and patterns, particularly those with scientific and mathematical significance.
- Genuine vs. Hoax Identification: To distinguish between genuine crop circles and hoaxes by employing advanced rating systems based on complexity, precision, and formation conditions.
- Scientific Interpretation: To develop a dictionary that translates the symbolic language of crop circles into scientific concepts, aiding in the understanding of potential messages from higher intelligences.

## Methodology

- Data Collection: Gather comprehensive data on crop circle formations worldwide, including high-resolution images, eyewitness accounts, and physical evidence.
- Pattern Analysis: Utilize advanced algorithms and machine learning techniques to identify and analyze recurring patterns and symbols within crop circles.
- Expert Collaboration: Collaborate with experts in various fields, including mathematics, physics, and semiotics, to interpret the scientific and symbolic meanings of crop circles.
- Rating System: Develop a robust rating system to assess the authenticity and significance of each crop circle, considering factors such as complexity, geometric precision, and formation conditions.

# BONUS CHAPTER: RECENT EVENTS - 2023 THE END OF A CYCLE & 2024 THE RISE OF THE MONOLITHS

The crop circle phenomenon has always been shrouded in mystery, with each season bringing new and intriguing formations. However, the years 2023 and 2024 have introduced unprecedented developments that suggest we might be witnessing the end of one cycle and the beginning of another. This chapter delves into the peculiar events of these years, including the conclusion of the 2023 crop circle season with a hydrogen signature and a recurrance of the "Led Zeppelin album cover" pattern, and the delayed 2024 season marked by the sudden appearance of hundreds of enigmatic silver monoliths.

## THE END OF THE 2023 CYCLE

**The Hydrogen Signature**
In a significant departure from the norm, the 2023 crop circle season concluded with a formation depicting a hydrogen atom, the simplest and most abundant element in the universe. This choice of symbol carries profound implications:
- Symbolic Meaning: Hydrogen, as the most fundamental building block of matter, symbolizes a beginning. Its appearance at the end of the season suggests a cycle's completion and a new genesis.
- Scientific Connection: Hydrogen is central to various scientific fields, including astronomy and chemistry. Its depiction could imply a connection to cosmic or elemental forces at play in the creation of crop circles.

**The "Led Zeppelin Album Cover" Formation**
The reappearance of the same pattern from 1990 at the end of the 2023 sseason also suggests the end of a cycle of some kind. We are still unsure as to the true meaning of this pattern, but it does seem to be important.

# THE MONOLITH PHENOMENON OF 2024

## A Delayed Crop Circle Season
2024 has been marked by an unusual delay in the crop circle season, which typically begins in early spring but this year did not start until July. This delay coincided with the emergence of a new and equally baffling phenomena:
- Absence of Early Formations: The expected springtime crop circles were notably absent, leading to speculation about the reasons behind the delay.
- Shift in Phenomena: The appearance of monoliths suggests a shift in the focus or methods of whatever intelligence or forces are behind the crop circle phenomena.

## The Appearance of Silver Monoliths
In place of the traditional crop circles, hundreds of silver monoliths have appeared worldwide. These monoliths exhibit several intriguing characteristics:
- Widespread Distribution: The monoliths have appeared in various locations, from remote fields to urban areas, suggesting a coordinated or global phenomena.
- Inscribed Patterns: Many of the monoliths are inscribed with patterns reminiscent of crop circles, linking the two phenomena and hinting at a shared origin or purpose.

## Potential Explanations
The appearance of these monoliths and the delayed crop circle season can be explored through several lenses:
- Technological Artifacts: The monoliths may represent a new form of communication or technology from the same intelligence responsible for crop circles.
- Symbolic Markers: The monoliths could serve as markers of significant locations or events, with their inscriptions providing clues to their purpose or origin.
- Human Imitation: Alternatively, these monoliths might be the work of human artists or pranksters inspired by the crop circle phenomena, adding a new layer of complexity to the mystery.

# YET ANOTHER LINK TO 2001 A SPACE ODYSSEY?

## INTERPRETATIONS & IMPLICATIONS

**The End of a Cycle**
The 2023 season's conclusion with a hydrogen signature and the recurring "Led Zeppelin album cover" pattern suggests the culmination of a significant cycle in the crop circle phenomenon.

A New Beginning: Just as hydrogen represents the beginning of matter, the end of this cycle might herald a new phase in the crop circle phenomena.

**The Monoliths and the Future**
The emergence of the monoliths in 2024 suggests a transformation or evolution in the phenomena:
- New Communication Methods: The shift from crop circles to monoliths could represent an advancement or change in how messages are being communicated.
- Broader Reach: The global distribution of the monoliths indicates a broader reach and potentially a more significant message or purpose.
Interdisciplinary Interest: The monolith phenomenon has captured the attention of not only crop circle enthusiasts but also artists, technologists, and the general public, indicating a wider impact and interest.

## RECENT EVENTS SUMMARY

The years 2023 and 2024 have marked a turning point in the crop circle phenomena. The end of the 2023 season with a hydrogen signature pattern and the unusual recurrance of the "Led Zeppelin cover" pattern, likely signals the conclusion of a significant cycle, while the delayed 2024 season and the emergence of hundreds of inscribed silver monoliths point to the beginning of a new chapter. These developments challenge our understanding and invite further investigation into the mysterious forces behind these enigmatic occurrences. As we continue to observe and study these phenomena, we may uncover deeper connections and insights into the interplay between human culture, cosmic forces, and mysterious intelligences.

## THANKS FOR READING! IF YOU FOUND THIS BOOK TO BE INSIGHTFUL, PLEASE GIVE IT A REVIEW :)

For centuries, crop circles have fascinated and perplexed humanity, appearing mysteriously in fields and sparking endless debates. Are they intricate works of art, elaborate hoaxes, or messages from a higher intelligence? In this groundbreaking research, we delve into the heart of the crop circle phenomena, exploring the most notable formations and the compelling evidence suggesting their otherworldly origins.

Discover the mysteries behind the Hydrogen Signature, the Arecibo Response, the enigmatic DNA disc, and a potential blueprint series. These formations challenge our understanding of communication and intelligence, offering potential proof of contact with advanced civilizations. This book raises critical questions about the likely dual nature of crop circles—man-made art versus signals from higher intelligence—and the sophisticated language conveyed.

Uncover the groundbreaking revelations that suggest we are not alone. Join us on this journey to decipher these extraordinary formations and uncover the potential messages they carry. Whether you're a seasoned researcher or a curious newcomer, this book will transform your understanding of crop circles and their significance.

## ABOUT THE AUTHOR

I'm Gavin Potts, dedicated researcher, programmer, graphic designer and now author with a deep fascination for unexplained phenomena and the potential implications of it. As the founder of The Crop Signals Project, I bring a unique perspective to the study of crop circles, combining my expertise in design, programming, mathematics and geometry and applying it to this intriguing subject.

My journey into the world of crop circles began in 2006 when a formation appeared in my home county of Norfolk, sparking my quest to uncover the hidden truths behind these enigmatic patterns. This innovative approach to crop circles seeks to decode the messages embedded within and encourage disclosure on the subject. With this book I hope to shed overdue light on what I think could in fact be a form of communication with a higher intelligence.

CROPSIGNALS.APP

© 2024 The Crop Signals Project

www.ingramcontent.com/pod-product-compliance
Lightning Source LLC
Chambersburg PA
CBHW070558160426
43199CB00014B/2542